D0779983

FREDERICK DOUGLASS

FREDERICK DOUGLASS

Charles Chesnutt

DOVER PUBLICATIONS, INC.
Mineola, New York

The photogravure used as a frontispiece to this volume is from a photograph by J. H. Kent, Rochester, New York, one of the last taken of Mr. Douglass. It is the portrait most highly thought of by his family, by whose permission it is used. The present engraving is by John Andrew & Son, Boston.

Copyright

"About the Author," "Background Notes," Introduction, editor's notes, and Index copyright © 2002 by Dover Publications.
All rights reserved.

Bibliographical Note

This Dover edition, first published in 2002, is an unabridged republication of the work originally published in 1899 by Small, Maynard & Company, Boston. "About the Author," "Background Notes," the Introduction, the editor's notes, and the index were added for the Dover edition.

Library of Congress Cataloging-in-Publication Data

Chesnutt, Charles Waddell, 1858-1932.
    Frederick Douglass I Charles Chesnutt. p.cm. Originally published: Boston : Small, Maynard, 1899, in series: The Beacon biographies of eminent Americans.
    Includes bibliographical references (p.).
    ISBN-13: 978 0-486-42254-1
    ISBN 0-486-42254-2 (pbk.)

    1. Douglass, Frederick, 1817?-1895. 2. African American abolitionists—Biography. 3. Abolitionists-United States-Biography. 4. Slaves-United States-Biography. 5. Antislavery movements-United States-History-19th century. I. Title.
    E449.D74985 2002
    973.8'092—d.c21
    [B]   2001047756

Manufactured in the United States by Courier Corporation
42254202
www.doverpublications.com

About the Author

Charles Waddell Chesnutt (1858–1932) was born in Cleveland, Ohio, in the year of the famous Oberlin, Ohio, rescue of escaped slaves (made necessary by the enforcement of the Fugitive Slave Act of 1850, which put all free African Americans living in the North in great danger of being enslaved). His parents had moved to the North when life in the South became completely untenable for free African Americans. In 1866 his parents returned to North Carolina, and Charles grew up in Fayetteville, during the danger and turmoil of Reconstruction. Chesnutt's father's father, like Frederick Douglass's father, was European-American—a plantation owner who fathered seven children with an enslaved woman. Chesnutt's mother also had mixed ancestry.

When he was fourteen Chesnutt began teaching in a school for African-American children. He married in 1878. Six years later he settled in Cleveland with his wife and their young children, after a brief stay in New York City in hopes of launching a literary career. He studied law and was accepted to practice as a lawyer in Ohio, but he actually supported his family as a court reporter. As Frederick Douglass noted, racism and the poverty of the vast majority of African Americans prevented the few well-educated African-American men from being able to prosper in any profession during the decades after the Civil War, as they could get neither European-American nor African-American clients.

Chesnutt's story "The Goophered Grapevine," published in the *Atlantic* magazine in 1887, was the first fiction by an African-American writer that received widespread attention from the European-American literary establishment and from European-

American readers. It revealed slave life on antebellum Southern plantations and explored African-American folk culture. In 1899, in addition to his biography of Frederick Douglass, two collections of Chesnutt's stories were published. *The Conjure Woman* was brought out in the spring by the prestigious Boston firm of Houghton Mifflin; *The Wife of His Youth and Other Stories of the Color Line* followed in the fall. During the next five years, three novels by Chesnutt that memorably exposed the human pain and the social costs of the U.S. heritage of chattel slavery—in particular, in relation to the "color line" so integral to the lives of people who had both European and African ancestry—were published. They were *The House Behind the Cedars* (1900), *The Marrow of Tradition* (1901), and *The Colonel's Dream* (1905).

After this intensively productive period very little of Chesnutt's fiction was published, but his work and its reception influenced and paved the way for the New Negro writers of the 1920s. In 1931, referring to the flourishing of African-American literary expression during the Harlem Renaissance, Chesnutt published the essay "Post-Bellum–Pre-Harlem," a retrospective look at his literary career.

Introduction

When Frederick Douglass arrived in New York City in September 1838 to begin life as a free man, he was entering a new and unknown world. It was not a world populated by contented people living in harmony. Even the privileged European-American males who formed the mercantile elite in the bustling port city were not having a good year.

Because young Frederick had spent quite a bit of time in the thriving Chesapeake Bay port of Baltimore (then the nation's second-largest city), and because he had learned to read, he had had some access to information regarding what was happening in other parts of the United States. From newspapers and accounts given by sailors, as well as from conversations overheard on the waterfront, he would have heard about major events and issues. However, communication and transportation methods still were slow in the far-flung and fast-growing country. (Samuel F.B. Morse made a preliminary filing for his telegraph at the U.S. Patent Office in the month of Frederick's arrival in New York, but an experimental line between Washington, D.C., and Baltimore was not built until 1844.) Frederick's knowledge of living conditions in the North must have been sketchy.

In 1833 President Andrew Jackson had achieved his longtime ambition of terminating the second Bank of the United States by withdrawing all federal funds from it. New banks, which came to be known as "pet banks," had been chartered in each state. In 1836 his Specie Circular had demanded that settlers pay for western land in gold or silver, not paper money. Over-wrought business activity, too-easy credit, and crop failures all contributed to a difficult economic situation triggered by the major changes in banking and monetary policy. A nationwide economic depression that began with the Panic of 1837 (hundreds of bank failures) had fully taken hold, in cities, towns, and farm areas alike and would last for nearly a decade.

In New York City, about 50,000 people had lost their jobs in 1837. An estimated 6,000 had participated in the Flour Riot that winter, invading a warehouse near the City Hall. The people of the city already were reeling from the effects of the Great Fire of December 1835, which had destroyed much of the oldest section of the city. A smaller but major fire in September 1833 had destroyed the Mother A.M.E. Zion church at the corner of Church and Leonard streets, but the African-American congregation soon had rebuilt it at the same site. (Unlike the owners of the National Theater and other buildings burned in the disaster, they had had the foresight to have it fully insured for fire damage.) In October 1833 the New York City Anti-Slavery Society had been founded, with philanthropic merchant Arthur Tappan as its first president. The home of his younger brother and business partner, Lewis, was wrecked by an anti-Abolitionist mob in July 1834.

In 1836 a Colored Orphan Asylum had been founded uptown on Twelfth Street by two European-American women, Mrs. Anna Shotwell and her niece. This probably was barely noticed by most New York City residents who were not African-American. The sensation of the year, especially among those European-American males who considered themselves to be "gentlemen about town," or aspired to be, was the gruesome ax-murder of Helen Jewett in her room at the house of prostitution run by inveterate Bible-reader Rosina Townsend, and the trial that followed. (The young clerk implicated by overwhelming evidence was acquitted.) In 1837, a third U.S. war with Great Britain had nearly begun, when young men in New York State went to the Canadian border to support a revolt in Quebec and Lower Canada. Poet William Cullen Bryant now was half-owner of the New York *Evening Post* and was working hard as editor to gain back readership and advertisers after a couple of difficult years. He opposed the annexation of Texas as a slaveholding state. (U.S. Southerners had bought land in Mexico, where slavery had been illegal since 1827, and then had won a small war against Mexican soldiers and established an independent slave-holding republic in 1836.) Scottish immigrant James Gordon Bennett had started the city's second penny daily newspaper, the New York *Herald,* in 1835 in time to cover the Great Fire and the Helen Jewett murder trial sensationally; he tended to support slavery, and anti-Catholic, nativist politicians.

New York City was by far the nation's largest, with more than 300,000 residents. Nearly 280,000 of them lived below 14th Street, though paved streets extended as far uptown as 42nd Street. Along the entire stretch of Broadway from the Bowling Green to Canal Street, the maelstrom of horse-drawn vehicles meant that it easily could take an hour for a person on foot to manage to cross from one side of the thoroughfare to the other. Since 1830, 12-passenger omnibuses had provided increasingly inexpensive if not necessarily comfortable public transportation along Broadway and a few other roads. Most of the African-American population was crowded into miserable wooden dwellings downtown, especially in and around the notorious Five Points slum and in the area around Carmine and Bleecker streets in Greenwich Village, which had been absorbed by the growing city. However, since 1825 a number of African-American families had established themselves, with churches and schools, in harmony with Irish-American and German-American neighbors, in Seneca Village, on farmland that later became part of Central Park, between 82nd and 86th streets, west of where the Croton reservoir later was built. John Hughes had arrived from Ireland in 1838 to assist the aging Bishop Dubois in leading the city's burgeoning Roman Catholic population. In the United States, the largely immigrant Catholic population was concentrated in the old port cities, while various Protestant denominations prevailed in rural areas. There were six or seven Irish Catholics in New York City for every German Catholic (the second largest group). The Native American Party, founded in 1837, was the first in a series of virulently anti-immigrant and anti-Catholic political parties. In 1836 artist Samuel F.B. Morse had gotten 1,500 votes as the Native-American candidate for mayor of New York City. Most people in the North who earned a living by manual labor on farms, in towns, or in cities did not want a lot of fugitive slaves from the South to compete with them and drive down wages for already low-paid jobs.

In New York State, all remaining slaves had been freed on July 4, 1827, after the effects of a gradual-manumission law passed in 1799 had freed most slaves. Around 1800, it has been estimated, about 40% of the householders in New York City and the surrounding area owned at least one slave. This was higher than the percentage of households in several Southern states that owned at least one slave. However, in New York State, as in New England, traditionally only one or two household slaves had been owned by each slaveholder, with the exception of owners of large farmlands in the Hudson Valley and in a few New England locations. David Ruggles, the African-American man who gave Frederick shelter upon his arrival in New York City, was a sailor who lived on Lispenard Street. He had become a bookseller and a publisher, as well as a leader in the effort to assist fugitive slaves.

William L. Marcy, who later originated the phrase "to the victor belong the spoils" in a U.S. Senate speech, still was governor of New York State in September 1838. He had held that office since 1833. However, William H. Seward was elected in 1838 to succeed him as governor. Isaac Varian, who followed a series of undistinguished men, would become mayor of New York City in 1839. The city was considered to be as unrivaled in the corruption of its government and the filth of its streets (where numerous pigs roamed and rooted) as it was in the prosperity of its merchants and financiers. During the social season, it was a favorite haunt of Southern plantation owners. Cotton was bought and sold exclusively by a few brokers in New York. On Christmas Eve, 1834, one of the city's richest men, Nat Prime, received the news from a just-docked ship, of which he was part owner, that the price of cotton had risen in Liverpool, England. An agent was sent to New Orleans with letters of credit for one million dollars and orders to buy cotton from growers before the news from England arrived via the Southern mail ship. The messenger reached New Orleans in eleven days, three days before the mail ship arrived. In one day, more than 50,000 bales of cotton were bought at about $60 a bale. That cotton soon was sold at a 50-percent profit. (The messenger was given the profits from the sale of 200 bales—about $6,000—as his compensation.) At that time, perhaps $10 was the typical amount spent to maintain a plantation slave for a year.

Many of the cargoes sold by New York's merchants on a grand scale came in on ships owned by New Englanders. Those vessels sailed from dozens of ports. Prominent among them were Portland and Bangor in Maine; Portsmouth in New Hampshire; Boston, Salem, New Bedford, and Newburyport in Massachusetts; Providence and Newport in Rhode Island; and New London, Norwich, and New Haven in Connecticut. Thus, New York City's businessmen had close ties with the prosperous men of both New England and the Southern states, and all three groups depended heavily on the slavery-based agricultural economy of the U.S. South and of the French- and Spanish-owned Caribbean islands, as well as the plantations in the British West Indies, where slavery recently had been ended.

In 1838 the United States of America was composed of 26 states. In at least half of them slave labor was basic to the economy and to the social order. Moreover, the current income and the inherited wealth of the prosperous and powerful class in New England and the Middle Atlantic states largely was based on the slave trade itself and on buying, refining, and reselling the products of plantations in the Southern states and in the Caribbean. Arkansas had become a state in June 1836, followed by Michigan in January 1837. Prior to 1836, no state had entered the Union since Missouri in 1821, preceded by Maine in 1820. Alabama had entered the Union in 1819, preceded by Illinois in 1818. Mississippi had become a state in 1817, preceded by Indiana (chiefly settled by Southerners) in 1816. These admissions to the Union had occurred in pairs, one slave state for each free state. Because of restrictive laws, no Northern state from Ohio west to Wisconsin was home to free African Americans amounting to even one percent of its population. In the older Northern states, riots and individual attacks on free African Americans by European Americans had been frequent occurrences since 1820. Such attacks were especially common in Philadelphia.

Earlier in 1838, the new Pennsylvania Hall in Philadelphia had been burned to the ground by a mob, soon after they stoned the 3,000 delegates to the Anti-slavery Convention of American Women, most of whom were European American. In the same year, the state of Pennsylvania denied the right to vote to all African-American men, even those who previously had been eligible because they met property-ownership requirements. In December 1838, talented English actress Fanny Kemble persuaded her husband, Pierce Butler, to let her accompany him from his Philadelphia mansion to the two Sea Island plantations off the coast of Georgia that he and his brother had inherited. The journal she kept during her four-month stay in Georgia, which unfortunately was not published until 1863, was as unique an account from the perspective of a European-American participant-observer as Frederick Douglass's 1845 *Narrative* was unique among the accounts theretofore published by former slaves.

By 1830 there were about 2 million African-American slaves in the United States (about 18% of the country's population). More than 200,000 free African Americans lived in the United States, mostly in the Northern states. When Frederick Douglass arrived in New York City in 1838, at least 10,000 free African Americans had been sent to the "colony" of Liberia in West Africa by the American Colonization Society, founded in 1817. However, the Society was nearing the end of its active period in sending African Americans to the continent of their ancestors. It had had a conflict-ridden history, as its supporters who sincerely wanted to benefit free African Americans were far outnumbered by the slaveholders (including U.S. presidents) who supported its activities because they simply wanted to "get rid of" the large numbers of free African Americans in the United States, whom they perceived as a menace to the slavery system and as generally undesirable members of society.

In 1829 David Walker, an African American, had issued his *Appeal to the Colored Citizens of the World,* an incitement to revolt which was carried to the South sewn into the lining of sailors' clothing sold in his Boston shop. Nat Turner's rebellion in Southampton County, Virginia, in August 1831 had aroused hatred and fear to a high pitch among slaveholders. From 1831 to 1833 Maria Stewart, an African American, was the first U.S. woman to give a series of public lectures (on how to improve the wellbeing of African Americans). Opposition to public speaking by a woman was so strong that she decided to limit herself to writing pamphlets, but she continued to work in the women's-suffrage movement and as an educator of African-American children. In 1833 the British had ended slavery in their colonies. They continued to use their navy to suppress the African slave trade, but slave traders still smuggled several thousand slaves into the U.S. South each year. Kidnappers also captured free African Americans in the North and sold them into plantation slavery. Also in 1833, the American Anti-slavery Society had been founded in Philadelphia by Abolitionists from ten states. William Lloyd Garrison wrote the Society's declaration of purpose. In that same year, Prudence Crandall, a Quaker, opened a free boarding school for African-American girls in Canterbury, Connecticut, after she was attacked for admitting an African-American young woman to her existing, successful school for the town's European-American girls. In 1834 she was forced to close the school and leave Connecticut, when her home was stoned and townspeople threatened to kill her students and burn the school. (Slavery effectively had been forbidden in Vermont—which did not become the 14th state until 1791—in 1777, and in Massachusetts by 1783, but it was not ended completely in New Jersey until 1846, in Connecticut until 1848, and in New Hampshire until 1857.)

About a year after Frederick Douglass arrived in New York City as an escaped slave and moved on to New Bedford, Massachusetts, the Cuban schooner *Amistad,* with dozens of newly enslaved Africans on board, who had rebelled and tried to sail back to their homeland, was captured by a U.S. Coast Guard ship off the coast of Long Island. President Martin Van Buren wanted to return the Africans to slavery in Cuba, but many New Englanders and others claimed the Africans' right to freedom. Former President John Quincy Adams defended the Africans when their case went to the U.S. Supreme Court in January 1841, and eventually the 36 men and 3 young women who had survived their shipboard sufferings and time in federal prisons were sent back to Africa.

Kathy Casey

New York, October 2001

Preface

Frederick Douglass lived so long, and played so conspicuous a part on the world's stage, that it would be impossible, in a work of the size of this, to do more than touch upon the salient features of his career, to suggest the respects in which he influenced the course of events in his lifetime, and to epitomize for the readers of another generation the judgment of his contemporaries as to his genius and his character.

Douglass's fame as an orator has long been secure. His position as the champion of an oppressed race, and at the same time an example of its possibilities, was, in his own generation, as picturesque as it was unique; and his life may serve for all time as an incentive to aspiring souls who would fight the battles and win the love of mankind. The average American of to-day who sees, when his attention is called to it, and deplores, if he be a thoughtful and just man, the deep undertow of race prejudice that retards the progress of the colored people of our own generation, cannot, except by reading the painful records of the past, conceive of the mental and spiritual darkness to which slavery, as the inexorable condition of its existence, condemned its victims and, in a less measure, their oppressors, or of the blank wall of proscription and scorn by which free people of color were shut up in a moral and social Ghetto, the gates of which have yet not been entirely torn down.

From this night of slavery Douglass emerged, passed through the limbo of prejudice which he encountered as a freeman, and took his place in history. "As few of the world's great men have ever had so checkered and diversified a career," says Henry Wilson, "so it may at least be plausibly claimed that no man represents in himself more conflicting ideas and interests. His life is, in itself, an epic which finds few to equal it in the realms of either romance or reality." It was, after all, no misfortune for humanity that Frederick Douglass felt the iron hand of slavery; for his genius changed the drawbacks of color and condition into levers by which he raised himself and his people.

The materials for this work have been near at hand, though there is a vast amount of which lack of space must prevent the use. Acknowledgment is here made to members of the Douglass family for aid in securing the photograph from which the frontispiece is reproduced.

The more the writer has studied the records of Douglass's life, the more it has appealed to his imagination and his heart. He can claim no special qualification for this task, unless perhaps it be a profound and in some degree a personal sympathy with every step of Douglass's upward career. Belonging to a later generation, he was only privileged to see the man and hear the orator after his life-work was substantially completed, but often enough then to appreciate something of the strength and eloquence by which he impressed his contemporaries. If by this brief sketch the writer can revive among the readers of another generation a tithe of the interest that Douglass created for himself when he led the forlorn hope of his race for freedom and opportunity, his labor will be amply repaid.

Charles W. Chesnutt

Cleveland, October, 1899

Chronology

1817
Frederick Douglass was born at Tuckahoe, near Easton, Talbot County, Maryland.

1825
Was sent to Baltimore to live with a relative of his master.

1833
March. Was taken to St. Michael's, Maryland, to live again with his master.

1834
January. Was sent to live with Edward Covey, slave-breaker, with whom he spent the year.

1835–36
Hired to William Freeland. Made an unsuccessful attempt to escape from slavery. Was sent to Baltimore to learn the ship-calker's trade.

1838
May. Hired his own time and worked at his trade.

September 3. Escaped from slavery and went to New York City. Married Miss Anna Murray. Went to New Bedford, Massachusetts. Assumed the name of "Douglass."

1841
Attended anti-slavery convention at New Bedford and addressed the meeting. Was employed as agent of the Massachusetts Anti-slavery Society.

1842
Took part in Rhode Island campaign against the Dorr constitution. Lectured on slavery. Moved to Lynn, Massachusetts.

1843
Took part in the famous "One Hundred Conventions" of the New England Anti-slavery Society.

1844

Lectured with Pillsbury, Foster, and others.

1845

Published *Frederick Douglass's Narrative.*

1845–46

Visited Great Britain and Ireland. Remained in Europe two years, lecturing on slavery and other subjects. Was presented by English friends with money to purchase his freedom and to establish a newspaper.

1847

Returned to the United States. Moved with his family to Rochester, New York. Established the *North Star,* subsequently renamed *Frederick Douglass's Paper.* Visited John Brown at Springfield, Massachusetts.

1848

Lectured on slavery and woman suffrage.

1849

Edited newspaper. Lectured against slavery. Assisted the escape of fugitive slaves.

1850

May 7. Attended meeting of Anti-slavery Society at New York City. Running debate with Captain Rynders.

1852

Supported the Free Soil party. Elected delegate from Rochester to Free Soil convention at Pittsburg, Pennsylvania. Supported John P. Hale for the Presidency.

1853

Visited Harriet Beecher Stowe at Andover, Massachusetts, with reference to industrial school for colored youth.

1854

Opposed repeal of Missouri Compromise.

June 12. Delivered commencement address at Western Reserve College, Hudson, Ohio.

1855

Published *My Bondage and My Freedom.*

March. Addressed the New York legislature.

1856

Supported Fremont, candidate of the Republican party.

1858

Established *Douglass's Monthly*. Entertained John Brown at Rochester.

1859

August 20. Visited John Brown at Chambersburg, Pennsylvania.

May 12 [October]. Went to Canada to avoid arrest for alleged complicity in the John Brown raid.

November 12. Sailed from Quebec for England.

Lectured and spoke in England and Scotland for six months.

1860

Returned to the United States. Supported Lincoln for the Presidency.

1862

Lectured and spoke in favor of the war and against slavery.

1863

Assisted in recruiting Fifty-fourth and Fifty-fifth Massachusetts colored regiments. Invited to visit President Lincoln.

1864

Supported Lincoln for re-election.

1866

Was active in procuring the franchise for the freedmen.

September. Elected delegate from Rochester to National Loyalists' Convention at Philadelphia.

1869 [1870]

Moved to Washington, District of Columbia. Established [Edited and then bought] the *New National Era*.

1870

Appointed secretary of the Santo Domingo Commission by President Grant.

1872

Appointed councillor of the District of Columbia. [Moved family there after a fire (probably arson) destroyed their Rochester home and Douglass's newspaper files.] Elected presidential elector of the State of New York, and chosen by the electoral college to take the vote to Washington.

1876

Delivered address at unveiling of Lincoln statue at Washington.

1877

Appointed Marshal of the District of Columbia by President Hayes.

1878

Visited his old home in Maryland and met his old master.

1879

Bust of Douglass placed in Sibley Hall, of Rochester University. Spoke against the proposed negro exodus from the South.

1881

Appointed recorder of deeds for the District of Columbia.

1882

January. Published *Life and Times of Frederick Douglass,* the third and last of his autobiographies.
August 4. Mrs. Frederick Douglass died.

1884

February 6. Attended funeral of Wendell Phillips. *February 9.* Attended memorial meeting and delivered eulogy on Phillips. Married Miss Helen Pitts.

1886

May 20. Lectured on John Brown at Music Hall, Boston.
September 11. Attended a dinner given in his honor by the Wendell Phillips Club, Boston.
September. Sailed for Europe.
Visited Great Britain, France, Italy, Greece, and Egypt, 1886–87.

1888

Made a tour of the Southern States.

1889

Appointed United States minister resident and consul-general to the Republic of Hayti and *chargé d'affaires* to Santo Domingo.

1890

September 22. Addressed abolition reunion at Boston.

1891

Resigned the office of minister to Hayti.

1893

Acted as commissioner for Hayti at World's Columbian Exposition.

1895

February 20. Frederick Douglass died at his home on Anacostia Heights, near Washington, District of Columbia.

Background Notes

Because publishers of the Beacon Biographies series, in which Charles Chesnutt's biography of Frederick Douglass originally was included, did not allow writers to use more than 20,000 words, the personal lives and relationships of the men about whom they wrote could not be presented in any detail. To clarify some points about people to whom Chesnutt alludes in this biography, the following brief background notes have been provided.

THE AULD FAMILY: Lucretia Auld was the only daughter of Captain Aaron Anthony, who owned Frederick Douglass during the boy's early childhood. Lucretia had two brothers. She became known as Lucretia Auld (first mentioned on page 7) when she married Thomas Auld (also first mentioned on page 7), the captain of a Chesapeake Bay sloop. As women had no property rights, her husband controlled any slaves she inherited. Thomas Auld let his brother, Hugh (first mentioned on page 4), who lived in Baltimore, have the young boy Frederick. Hugh's wife was Sophia Auld. Their son, named Thomas (Tommy), was younger than Frederick. The "family misunderstanding" mentioned on page 7 was that Thomas Auld became angry at his brother, Hugh, and took Frederick away from Hugh's household in Baltimore. Lucretia Auld died not long after inheriting Frederick at her father's death. She left one child, Amanda, who is the woman mentioned on page 45, though her name is not given in Chesnutt's biography. It seems likely that the Thomas Auld mentioned on page 54 is the boy Tommy, whom Frederick was assigned to care for when both were children, not the boy's uncle, who sent the teenager Frederick to the slave-breaker Edward Covey. "The good lady . . . who taught him to read," also mentioned on page 54, is Sophia Auld.

THE DOUGLASS FAMILY: Frederick Douglass had at least three enslaved sisters and one enslaved brother, that he knew of (children of his

xxi

mother). As mentioned in the Chronology on page xvii, the free woman from Baltimore whom Frederick Douglass married in New York City in September 1838 was Anna Murray (page 10). The couple had five children, two girls and three boys. They were Rosetta (born 1839), Lewis (born 1840), Frederick (born 1842, died 1892), Charles (born 1844), and Annie (born 1849, died 1860; mentioned on page 38). Douglass's second wife (mentioned on page 54) was his secretary prior to their marriage, two years after he was widowed.

JAMES MONROE AND HIS FAMILY: The James Monroe who is identified in footnotes on pages 15 and 17 was almost the only European-American Abolitionist who accompanied Douglass in sleeping, fully clothed, in any weather, on steamboat decks, because African Americans were not allowed to enter steamboat cabins or to sleep anywhere except on the open deck. Monroe married in 1847. Like Douglass and his wife, he and his wife had five children and one of their daughters died in childhood. Monroe was a little younger than Douglass and died three years after his friend. Like Douglass, he was active and influential until the end of his life.

THE HUTCHINSON FAMILY: Mentioned on pages 21 and 56, the Hutchinson family of singers for social justice was from New Hampshire and included Judson, John, Asa, and Abby.

SOJOURNER TRUTH: This famous crusader (1797?–1883) against slavery and for the rights of women was known as Isabella Van Wagener after she was freed in 1827 from three decades of slavery in New York State. Some of her children had been taken from her and sold into slavery in the South. From 1827 onward, she preached true Christianity on the streets of New York City. Beginning in 1843, she spoke in public in Northern states on behalf of the Abolitionist movement and of women's rights.

✿   ✿   ✿   ✿   ✿

In a few places in the text of *Frederick Douglass*, bracketed words have been inserted to indicate possible typographical errors, other unclear or misleading passages in the 1899 original edition, and identifications that were not needed in 1899 but may be needed in the twenty-first century.

I.

If it be no small task for a man of the most favored antecedents and the most fortunate surroundings to rise above mediocrity in a great nation, it is surely a more remarkable achievement for a man of the very humblest origin possible to humanity in any country in any age of the world, in the face of obstacles seemingly insurmountable, to win high honors and rewards, to retain for more than a generation the respect of good men in many lands, and to be deemed worthy of enrolment among his country's great men. Such a man was Frederick Douglass, and the example of one who thus rose to eminence by sheer force of character and talents that neither slavery nor caste proscription could crush must ever remain as a shining illustration of the essential superiority of manhood to environment. Circumstances made Frederick Douglass a slave, but they could not prevent him from becoming a freeman and a leader among mankind.

The early life of Douglass, as detailed by himself from the platform in vigorous and eloquent speech, and as recorded in the three volumes written by himself at different periods of his career, is perhaps the completest indictment of the slave system ever presented at the bar of public opinion. Fanny Kemble's *Journal of a Residence on a Georgian Plantation*, kept by her in the very year of Douglass's escape from bondage, but not published until 1863, too late to contribute anything to the downfall of slavery is a singularly clear revelation of plantation life from the standpoint of an outsider entirely unbiased by American prejudice. *Frederick Douglass's Narrative* is the same story told from the inside. They coincide in the main facts; and in the matter of detail, like the two slightly differing views of a stereoscopic picture, they bring out into bold relief the real character of the peculiar institution. *Uncle Tom's Cabin* lent to the structure of fact the decorations of humor, a dramatic plot, and characters to whose fate the touch of creative genius gave a living interest. But, after all, it was not Uncle Tom, nor Topsy, nor Miss Ophelia, nor Eliza, nor little Eva that made the book the power it proved to stir the hearts of men, but the great underlying tragedy then already rapidly approaching a bloody climax.

Frederick Douglass was born in February, 1817,—as nearly as the date could be determined in after years, when it became a matter of public interest,—at Tuckahoe, near Easton, Talbot County, on the eastern shore of Maryland, a barren and poverty-stricken district, which possesses in the birth of Douglass its sole title to distinction. His mother was a negro slave, tall, erect, and well-proportioned, of a deep black and glossy complexion, with regular features, and manners of a natural dignity and sedateness. Though a field hand and compelled to toil many hours a day, she had in some mysterious way learned to read, being the only person of color in Tuckahoe, slave or free, who possessed that accomplishment. His father was a white man. It was in the nature of things that in after years attempts should be made to analyze the sources of Douglass's talent, and that the question should be raised whether he owed it to the black or the white half of his mixed ancestry. But Douglass himself, who knew his own mother and grandmother, ascribed such powers as he possessed to the negro half of his blood; and, as to it certainly he owed the experience which gave his anti-slavery work its peculiar distinction and value, he doubtless believed it only fair that the credit for what he accomplished should go to those who needed it most and could justly be proud of it. He never knew with certainty who his white father was, for the exigencies of slavery separated the boy from his mother before the subject of his paternity became of interest to him; and in after years his white father never claimed the honor, which might have given him a place in history.

Douglass's earliest recollections centered around the cabin of his grandmother, Betsey Bailey, who seems to have been something of a privileged character on the plantation, being permitted to live with her husband, Isaac, in a cabin of their own, charged with only the relatively light duty of looking after a number of young children, mostly the offspring of her own five daughters, and providing for her own support.

It is impossible in a work of the scope of this to go into very elaborate detail with reference to this period of Douglass's life, however interesting it might be. The real importance of his life to us of another generation lies in what he accomplished toward the world's progress, which he only began to influence several years after his escape from slavery. Enough ought to be stated, however, to trace his development from slave to freeman, and his preparation for the platform where he secured his hearing and earned his fame.

Douglass was born the slave of one Captain Aaron Anthony, a man of some consequence in eastern Maryland, the manager or chief clerk of one Colonel Lloyd, the head for that generation of an old, exceedingly wealthy, and highly honored family in Maryland, the possessor of a stately mansion and one of the largest and most fertile plantations in the State. Captain Anthony, though only the satellite of this great man, himself owned several farms and a number of slaves. At the age of seven Douglass was taken from the cabin of his grandmother at Tuckahoe to his master's residence on Colonel Lloyd's plantation.

Up to this time he had never, to his recollection, seen his mother. All his impressions of her were derived from a few brief visits made to him at Colonel Lloyd's plantation, most of them at night. These fleeting visits of the mother were important events in the life of the child, now no longer under the care of his grandmother, but turned over to the tender mercies of his master's cook, with whom he does not seem to have been a favorite. His mother died when he was eight or nine years old. Her son did not see her during her illness, nor learn of it until after her death. It was always a matter of grief to him that he did not know her better, and that he could not was one of the sins of slavery that he never forgave.

On Colonel Lloyd's plantation Douglass spent four years of the slave life of which his graphic description on the platform stirred humane hearts to righteous judgment of an unrighteous institution. It is enough to say that this lad, with keen eyes and susceptible feelings, was an eye-witness of all the evils to which slavery gave birth. Its extremes of luxury and misery could be found within the limits of one estate. He saw the field hand driven forth at dawn to labor until dark. He beheld every natural affection crushed when inconsistent with slavery, or warped and distorted to fit the necessities and promote the interests of the institution. He heard the unmerited strokes of the lash on the backs of others, and felt them on his own. In the wild songs of the slaves he read, beneath their senseless jargon or their fulsome praise of "old master," the often unconscious note of grief and despair. He perceived, too, the debasing effects of slavery upon master and slave alike, crushing all semblance of manhood in the one, and in the other substituting passion for judgment, caprice for justice, and indolence and effeminacy for the more virile virtues of freemen. Doubtless the gentle hand of time will some time spread the veil of silence over this painful past; but, while we are still gathering its evil aftermath, it is well enough that we do not forget the origin of so many of our civic problems.

When Douglass was ten years old, he was sent from the Lloyd plantation to Baltimore, to live with one Hugh Auld, a relative of his master. Here he enjoyed the high privilege, for a slave, of living in the house with his master's family. In the capacity of house boy it was his duty to run errands and take care of a little white boy, Tommy Auld, the son of his mistress for the time being, Mrs. Sophia Auld. Mrs. Auld was of a religious turn of mind; and, from hearing her reading the Bible aloud frequently, curiosity prompted the boy to ask her to teach him to read. She complied, and found him an apt pupil, until her husband learned of her unlawful and dangerous conduct, and put an end to the instruction. But the evil was already done, and the seed thus sown brought forth fruit in the after career of the orator and leader of men. The mere fact that his master wished to prevent his learning made him all the more eager to acquire knowledge. In after years, even when most bitter in his denunciation of the palpable evils of slavery, Douglass always acknowledged the debt he owed to this good lady who innocently broke the laws and at the same time broke the chains that held a mind in bondage.

Douglass lived in the family of Hugh Auld at Baltimore for seven years. During this time the achievement that had the greatest influence upon his future was his learning to read and write. His mistress had given him a start. His own efforts gained the rest. He carried in his pocket a blue-backed *Webster's Spelling Book,* and, as occasion offered, induced his young white playmates, by the bribes of childhood, to give him lessons in spelling. When he was about thirteen, he began to feel deeply the moral yoke of slavery and to seek for knowledge of the means to escape it. One book seems to have had a marked influence upon his life at this epoch. He obtained, somehow, a copy of *The Columbian Orator,* containing some of the choicest masterpieces of English oratory, in which he saw liberty praised and oppression condemned; and the glowing periods of Pitt and Fox and Sheridan and our own Patrick Henry stirred to life in the heart of this slave boy the genius for oratory which did not burst forth until years afterward. The worldly wisdom of denying to slaves the key to knowledge is apparent when it is said that Douglass first learned from a newspaper that there were such people as abolitionists, who were opposed to human bondage and sought to make all men free. At about this same period Douglass's mind fell under religious influences. He was converted, professed faith in Jesus Christ, and began to read the Bible. He had dreamed of liberty before: he now prayed for it, and trusted in God. But, with the shrewd common sense which marked his whole life and saved it from shipwreck in more than one instance, he never forgot that God helps them that help themselves, and so never missed an opportunity to acquire the knowledge that would prepare him for freedom and give him the means of escape from slavery.

Douglass had learned to read, partly from childish curiosity and the desire to be able to do what others around him did; but it was with a definite end in view that he learned to write. By the slave code it was unlawful for a slave to go beyond the limits of his own neighborhood without the written permission of his master. Douglass's desire to write grew mainly out of the fact that in order to escape from bondage, which he had early determined to do, he would probably need such a "pass," as this written permission was termed, and could write it himself if he but knew how. His master for the time being kept a ship-yard, and in this and neighboring establishments of the same kind the boy spent much of his time. He noticed that the carpenters, after dressing pieces of timber, marked them with certain letters to indicate their positions in the vessel. By asking questions of the workmen he learned the names of these letters and their significance. He got up writing matches with sticks upon the ground with the little white boys, copied the italics in his spelling-book, and in the secrecy of the attic filled up all the blank spaces of his young master's old copy-books. In time he learned to write, and thus again demonstrated the power of the mind to overleap the bounds that men set for it and work out the destiny to which God designs it.

II.

It was the curious fate of Douglass to pass through almost every phase of slavery, as though to prepare him the more thoroughly for his future career. Shortly after he went to Baltimore, his master, Captain Anthony, died intestate, and his property was divided between his two children. Douglass, with the other slaves, was part of the personal estate, and was sent for to be appraised and disposed of in the division. He fell to the share of Mrs. Lucretia Auld, his master's daughter, who sent him back to Baltimore, where, after a month's absence, he resumed his life in the household of Mrs. Hugh Auld, the sister-in-law of his legal mistress. Owing to a family misunderstanding, he was taken, in March, 1833, from Baltimore back to St. Michael's.

His mistress, Lucretia Auld, had died in the mean time; and the new household in which he found himself, with Thomas Auld and his second wife, Rowena, at its head, was distinctly less favorable to the slave boy's comfort than the home where he had lived in Baltimore. Here he saw hardships of the life in bondage that had been less apparent in a large city. It is to be feared that Douglass was not the ideal slave, governed by the meek and lowly spirit of Uncle Tom. He seems, by his own showing, to have manifested but little appreciation of the wise oversight, the thoughtful care, and the freedom from responsibility with which slavery claimed to hedge round its victims, and he was inclined to spurn the rod rather than to kiss it. A tendency to insubordination, due partly to the freer life he had led in Baltimore, got him into disfavor with a master easily displeased; and, not proving sufficiently amenable to the discipline of the home plantation, he was sent to a certain celebrated negro-breaker by the name of Edward Covey, one of the poorer whites who, as overseers and slave-catchers, and in similar unsavory capacities, earned a living as parasites on the system of slavery. Douglass spent a year under Covey's ministrations, and his life there may be summed up in his own words: "I had neither sufficient time in which to eat nor to sleep, except on Sundays. The overwork and the brutal chastisements of which I was the victim, combined with that ever-gnawing and soul-destroying thought, 'I am a slave,—a slave for life,' rendered me a living embodiment of mental and physical wretchedness."

But even all this did not entirely crush the indomitable spirit of a man destined to achieve his own freedom and thereafter to help win freedom for a race. In August, 1834, after a particularly atrocious beating, which left him wounded and weak from loss of blood, Douglass escaped the vigilance of the slave-breaker and made his way back to his own master to seek protection. The master, who would have lost his slave's wages for a year if he had broken the contract with Covey before the year's end, sent Douglass back to his taskmaster. Anticipating the most direful consequences, Douglass made the desperate resolution to resist any further punishment at Covey's hands. After a fight of two hours Covey gave up his attempt to whip Frederick, and thenceforth laid hands on him no more. That Covey did not invoke the law, which made death the punishment of the slave who resisted his master, was probably due to shame at having been worsted by a negro boy, or to the prudent consideration that there was no profit to be derived from a dead negro. Strength of character, re-enforced by strength of muscle, thus won a victory over brute force that secured for Douglass comparative immunity from abuse during the remaining months of his year's service with Covey.

The next year, 1835, Douglass was hired out to a Mr. William Freeland, who lived near St. Michael's, a gentleman who did not forget justice or humanity, so far as they were consistent with slavery, even in dealing with bond-servants. Here Douglass led a comparatively comfortable life. He had enough to eat, was not overworked, and found the time to conduct a surreptitious Sunday-school, where he tried to help others by teaching his fellow-slaves to read the Bible.

III.

The manner of Douglass's escape from Maryland was never publicly disclosed by him until the war had made slavery a memory and the slave-catcher a thing of the past. It was the theory of the anti-slavery workers of the time that the publication of the details of escapes or rescues from bondage seldom reached the ears of those who might have learned thereby to do likewise, but merely furnished the master class with information that would render other escapes more difficult and bring suspicion or punishment upon those who had assisted fugitives. That this was no idle fear there is abundant testimony in the annals of the period. But in later years, when there was no longer any danger of unpleasant consequences, and when it had become an honor rather than a disgrace to have assisted a distressed runaway, Douglass published in detail the story of his flight. It would not compare in dramatic interest with many other celebrated escapes from slavery or imprisonment. He simply masqueraded as a sailor, borrowed a sailor's "protection," or certificate that he belonged to the navy, took the train to Baltimore in the evening, and rode in the negro car until he reached New York City. There were many anxious moments during this journey. The "protection" he carried described a man somewhat different from him, but the conductor did not examine it carefully. Fear clutched at the fugitive's heart whenever he neared a State border line. He saw several persons whom he knew; but, if they recognized him or suspected his purpose, they made no sign. A little boldness, a little address, and a great deal of good luck carried him safely to his journey's end.

Douglass arrived in New York on September 4, 1838, having attained only a few months before what would have been in a freeman his legal majority. But, though landed in a free State, he was by no means a free man. He was still a piece of property, and could be reclaimed by the law's aid if his whereabouts were discovered. While local sentiment at the North afforded a measure of protection to fugitives, and few were ever returned to bondage compared with the number that escaped, yet the fear of recapture was ever with them, darkening their lives and impeding their pursuit of happiness.

But even the partial freedom Douglass had achieved gave birth to a thousand delightful sensations. In his autobiography he describes this dawn of liberty thus:—

"A new world had opened up to me. I lived more in one day than in a year of my slave life. I felt as one might feel upon escape from a den of hungry lions. My chains were broken, and the victory brought me unspeakable joy."

But one cannot live long on joy; and, while his chains were broken, he was not beyond the echo of their clanking. He met on the streets, within a few hours after his arrival in New York, a man of his own color, who informed him that New York was full of Southerners at that season of the year, and that slave-hunters and spies were numerous, that old residents of the city were not safe, and that any recent fugitive was in imminent danger. After this cheerful communication Douglass's informant left him, evidently fearing that Douglass himself might be a slave-hunting spy. There were negroes base enough to play this rôle. In a sailor whom he encountered he found a friend. This Good Samaritan took him home for the night, and accompanied him next day to a Mr. David Ruggles, a colored man, the secretary of the New York Vigilance Committee and an active antislavery worker. Mr. Ruggles kept him concealed for several days, during which time the woman Douglass loved, a free woman, came on from Baltimore; and they were married. He had no money in his pocket, and nothing to depend upon but his hands, which doubtless seemed to him quite a valuable possession, as he knew they had brought in an income of several hundred dollars a year to their former owner.

Douglass's new friends advised him to go to New Bedford, Massachusetts, where whaling fleets were fitted out, and where he might hope to find work at his trade of ship-calker. It was believed, too, that he would be safer there, as the anti-slavery sentiment was considered too strong to permit a fugitive slave's being returned to the South.

When Douglass, accompanied by his wife, arrived in New Bedford, a Mr. Nathan Johnson, a colored man to whom he had been recommended, received him kindly, gave him shelter and sympathy, and lent him a small sum of money to redeem his meagre baggage, which had been held by the stage-driver as security for an unpaid balance of the fare to New Bedford. In his autobiography Douglass commends Mr. Johnson for his "noble-hearted hospitality and manly character."

In New York Douglass had changed his name in order the better to hide his identity from any possible pursuer. Douglass's name was another tie that bound him to his race. He has been called "Douglass" by the writer because that was the name he took for himself, as he did his education and his freedom; and as "Douglass" he made himself famous. As a slave, he was legally entitled to but one name,—Frederick. From his grandfather, Isaac Bailey, a freeman, he had derived the surname Bailey. His mother, with unconscious sarcasm, had called the little slave boy Frederick Augustus Washington Bailey. The bearer of this imposing string of appellations had, with a finer sense of fitness, cut it down to Frederick Bailey. In New York he had called himself Frederick Johnson; but, finding when he reached New Bedford that a considerable portion of the colored population of the city already rejoiced in this familiar designation, he fell in with the suggestion of his host, who had been reading Scott's *Lady of the Lake*, and traced an analogy between the runaway slave and the fugitive chieftain, that the new freeman should call himself Douglass, after the noble Scot of that name [Douglas]. The choice proved not inappropriate, for this modern Douglass fought as valiantly in his own cause and with his own weapons as ever any Douglass [Douglas] fought with flashing steel in border foray.

Here, then, in a New England town, Douglass began the life of a freeman, from which, relieved now of the incubus of slavery, he soon emerged into the career for which, in the providence of God, he seemed by his multiform experience to have been especially fitted. He did not find himself, even in Massachusetts, quite beyond the influence of slavery. While before the law of the State he was the equal of any other man, caste prejudice prevented him from finding work at his trade of calker; and he therefore sought employment as a laborer. This he found easily, and for three years worked at whatever his hands found to do. The hardest toil was easy to him, the heaviest burdens were light; for the money that he earned went into his own pocket. If it did not remain there long, he at least had the satisfaction of spending it and of enjoying what it purchased.

During these three years he was learning the lesson of liberty and unconsciously continuing his training for the work of an anti-slavery agitator. He became a subscriber to the *Liberator,* each number of which he devoured with eagerness. He heard William Lloyd Garrison lecture, and became one of his most devoted disciples. He attended every anti-slavery meeting in New Bedford, and now and then spoke on the subject of slavery in humble gatherings of his own people.

IV.

In 1841 Douglass entered upon that epoch of his life which brought the hitherto obscure refugee prominently before the public, and in which his services as anti-slavery orator and reformer constitute his chief claim to enduring recollection. Millions of negroes whose lives had been far less bright than Douglass's had lived and died in slavery. Thousands of fugitives under assumed names were winning a precarious livelihood in the free States and trembling in constant fear of the slave-catcher. Some of these were doing noble work in assisting others to escape from bondage. Mr. Siebert, in his *Underground Railroad*, mentions one fugitive slave, John Mason by name, who assisted thirteen hundred others to escape from Kentucky. Another picturesque fugitive was Harriet Tubman, who devoted her life to this work with a courage, skill, and success that won her a wide reputation among the friends of freedom. A number of free colored men in the North, a few of them wealthy and cultivated, lent their time and their means to this cause. But it was reserved for Douglass, by virtue of his marvellous gift of oratory, to become pre-eminently the personal representative of his people for a generation.

In 1841 the Massachusetts Anti-slavery Society, which had been for some little time weakened by faction, arranged its differences, and entered upon a campaign of unusual activity, which found expression in numerous meetings throughout the free States, mainly in New England. On August 15 of that year a meeting was held at Nantucket, Massachusetts. The meeting was conducted by John A. Collins, at that time general agent of the society, and was addressed by William Lloyd Garrison and other leading abolitionists. Douglass had taken a holiday and come from New Bedford to attend this convention, without the remotest thought of taking part except as a spectator. The proceedings were interesting, and aroused the audience to a high state of feeling. There was present in the meeting a certain abolitionist, by name William C. Coffin, who had heard Douglass speak in the little negro Sunday-school at New Bedford, and who knew of his recent escape from slavery. To him came the happy inspiration to ask Douglass to speak a few words to the convention by way of personal testimony. Collins introduced the speaker as "a graduate from slavery, with his diploma written upon his back."

Douglass himself speaks very modestly about this, his first public appearance. He seems, from his own account, to have suffered somewhat from stage fright, which was apparently his chief memory concerning it. The impressions of others, however, allowing a little for the enthusiasm of the moment, are a safer guide as to the effect of Douglass's first speech. Parker Pillsbury reported that, "though it was late in the evening when the young man closed his remarks, none seemed to know or care for the hour. . . . The crowded congregation had been wrought up almost to enchantment during the whole long evening, particularly by some of the utterances of the last speaker [Douglass], as he turned over the terrible apocalypse of his experience in slavery." Mr. Garrison bore testimony to "the extraordinary emotion it exerted on his own mind and to the powerful impression it exerted upon a crowded auditory." "Patrick Henry," he declared, "had never made a more eloquent speech than the one they had just listened to from the lips of the hunted fugitive." Upon Douglass and his speech as a text Mr. Garrison delivered one of the sublimest and most masterly efforts of his life; and then and there began the friendship between the fugitive slave and the great agitator which opened the door for Douglass to a life of noble usefulness, and secured to the anti-slavery cause one of its most brilliant and effective orators.

At Garrison's instance Collins offered Douglass employment as lecturer for the Anti-slavery Society, though the idea of thus engaging him doubtless occurred to more than one of the abolition leaders who heard his Nantucket speech. Douglass was distrustful of his own powers. Only three years out of slavery, with little learning and no experience as a public speaker, painfully aware of the prejudice which must be encountered by men of his color, fearful too of the publicity that might reveal his whereabouts to his legal owner, who might reclaim his property wherever found, he yielded only reluctantly to Mr. Collins's proposition, and agreed at first upon only a three months' term of service. Most of the abolitionists were, or meant to be, consistent in their practice of what they preached; and so, when Douglass was enrolled as one of the little band of apostles, they treated him literally as a man and a brother. Their homes, their hearts, and their often none too well-filled purses were open to him. In this new atmosphere his mind expanded, his spirit took on high courage, and he read and studied diligently, that he might make himself worthy of his opportunity to do something for his people.

During the remainder of 1841 Douglass travelled and lectured in Eastern Massachusetts with George Foster, in the interest of the two leading abolition journals, the *Anti-slavery Standard* and the *Liberator,* and also lectured in Rhode Island against the proposed Dorr constitution, which sought to limit the right of s-uffrage to white male citizens only, thus disfranchising colored men who had theretofore voted. With Foster and Pillsbury and Parker[1] and Monroe[2] and Abby Kelly [Kelley][3] he labored to defeat the Dorr constitution and at the same time promote the abolition gospel. The proposed constitution was defeated, and colored men who could meet the Rhode Island property qualification were left in possession of the right to vote.

Douglass had plunged into this new work, after the first embarrassment wore off, with all the enthusiasm of youth and hope. But, except among the little band of Garrisonians and their sympathizers, his position did not relieve him from the disabilities attaching to his color. The feeling toward the negro in New

---

[1] Editor's Note to Dover Edition: Reverend Theodore Parker (1810–1860) was a Unitarian minister who graduated from the Harvard Divinity School and was active in the Boston area.

[2] Editor's Note to Dover Edition: James Monroe (1821–1898), a New Englander with a Quaker mother; in 1839 he became an Abolitionist lecturer instead of enrolling in college

[3] Editor's Note to Dover Edition: Abigail Kelley Foster (1811–1887), who married another Abolitionist, Stephen Foster, in 1845, was a Quaker orator and organizer on behalf of the abolition of slavery and for women's right to vote.

England in 1841 was but little different from that in the State of Georgia to-day. Men of color were regarded and treated as belonging to a distinctly inferior order of creation. At hotels and places of public resort they were refused entertainment. On railroads and steamboats they were herded off by themselves in mean and uncomfortable cars. If welcomed in churches at all, they were carefully restricted to the negro pew. As in the Southern States to-day, no distinction was made among them in these respects by virtue of dress or manners or culture or means; but all were alike discriminated against because of their dark skins. Some of Douglass's abolition friends, among whom he especially mentions Wendell Phillips and two others of lesser note, won their way to his heart by at all times refusing to accept privileges that were denied to their swarthy companion. Douglass resented proscription wherever met with, and resisted it with force when the odds were not too overwhelming. More than once he was beaten and maltreated by railroad conductors and brakemen. For a time the Eastern Railroad ran its cars through Lynn, Massachusetts, without stopping, because Douglass, who resided at that time in Lynn, insisted on riding in the white people's car, and made trouble when interfered with. Often it was impossible for the abolitionists to secure a meeting-place; and in several instances Douglass paraded the streets with a bell, like a town crier, to announce that he would lecture in the open air.

Some of Douglass's friends, it must be admitted, were at times rather extreme in their language, and perhaps stirred up feelings that a more temperate vocabulary would not have aroused. None of them ever hesitated to call a spade a spade, and some of them denounced slavery and all its sympathizers with the vigor and picturesqueness of a Muggletonian or Fifth Monarchy man of Cromwell's time execrating his religious adversaries. And, while it was true enough that the Church and the State were, generally speaking, the obsequious tools of slavery, it was not easy for an abolitionist to say so in vehement language without incurring the charge of treason or blasphemy,—an old trick of bigotry and tyranny to curb freedom of thought and freedom of speech. The little personal idiosyncrasies which some of the reformers affected, such as long hair in the men and short hair in the women,—there is surely some psychological reason why reformers run to such things,—served as convenient excuses for gibes and unseemly interruptions at their public meetings. On one memorable occasion, at Syracuse, New York, in November, 1842, Douglass and his fellows narrowly escaped tar and feathers. But, although Douglass was vehemently denunciatory of slavery in all its aspects, his twenty years of training in that hard school had developed in him a vein of prudence that saved him from these verbal excesses,—perhaps there was also some element of taste involved,—and thus made his arguments more effective than if he had alienated his audiences by indiscriminate attacks on all the institutions of society. No one could justly accuse Frederick Douglass of cowardice or self-seeking; yet he was opportunist enough to sacrifice the immaterial for the essential, and to use the best means at hand to promote the ultimate object sought, although the means thus offered might not be the ideal instrument. It was doubtless this trait that led Douglass, after he separated from his abolitionist friends, to modify his views upon the subject of disunion and the constitutionality of slavery, and to support political parties whose platforms by no means expressed the full measure of his convictions.

In 1843 the New England Anti-slavery Society resolved, at its annual meeting in the spring, to stir the Northern heart and rouse the national conscience by a series of one hundred conventions in New Hampshire, Vermont, New York, Ohio, Indiana, and Pennsylvania. Douglass was assigned as one of the agents for the conduct of this undertaking. Among those associated in this work, which extended over five months, were John A. Collins, the president of the society, who mapped out the campaign; James Monroe;[1] George Bradburn; William A. White, Charles L. Remond,[2] a colored orator, born in Massachusetts,

---

[1] Editor's Note to Dover Edition: In 1844 Monroe moved to Ohio, where he earned two degrees at Oberlin College and then taught there. He was an Ohio state legislator in the 1850s, U.S. Consul to slaveholding Brazil 1862–1869, and a U.S. Congressman during the 1870s.

[2] Editor's Note to Dover Edition: Remond (1810–1873), born free in Salem, Massachusetts, was the first African-American to address Abolitionist meetings.

who rendered effective service in the abolition cause; and Sidney Howard Gay, at that time managing editor of the *National Anti-slavery Standard* and later of the New York *Tribune* and the New York *Evening Post.*

The campaign upon which this little band of missionaries set out was no inconsiderable one. They were not going forth to face enthusiastic crowds of supporters, who would meet them with brass bands and shouts of welcome. They were more likely to be greeted with hisses and cat-calls, sticks and stones, stale eggs and decayed cabbages, hoots and yells of derision, and decorations of tar and feathers.

In some towns of Vermont slanderous reports were made in advance of their arrival, their characters were assailed, and their aims and objects misrepresented. In Syracuse, afterward distinguished for its strong anti-slavery sentiment, the abolitionists were compelled to hold their meetings in the public park, from inability to procure a house in which to speak; and only after their convention was well under way were they offered the shelter of a dilapidated and abandoned church. In Rochester they met with a more hospitable reception. The indifference of Buffalo so disgusted Douglass's companions that they shook the dust of the city from their feet, and left Douglass, who was accustomed to coldness and therefore undaunted by it, to tread the wine-press alone. He spoke in an old post-office for nearly a week, to such good purpose that a church was thrown open to him; and on a certain Sunday, in the public park, he held and thrilled by his eloquence an audience of five thousand people.

On leaving Buffalo, Douglass joined the other speakers, and went with them to Clinton County, Ohio, where, under a large tent, a mass meeting was held of abolitionists who had come from widely scattered points. During an excursion made about this time to Pennsylvania to attend a convention at Norristown, an attempt was made to lynch him at Manayunk; but his usual good fortune served him, and he lived to be threatened by higher powers than a pro-slavery mob.

When the party of reformers reached Indiana, where the pro-slavery spirit was always strong, the State having been settled largely by Southerners, their campaign of education became a running fight, in which Douglass, whose dark skin attracted most attention, often got more than his share. His strength and address brought him safely out of many an encounter; but in a struggle with a mob at Richmond, Indiana, he was badly beaten and left unconscious on the ground. A good Quaker took him home in his wagon, his wife bound up Douglass's wounds and nursed him tenderly,—the Quakers were ever the consistent friends of freedom,—but for the lack of proper setting he carried to the grave a stiff hand as the result of this affray. He had often been introduced to audiences as "a graduate from slavery with his diploma written upon his back": from Indiana he received the distinction of a post-graduate degree.

V.

It can easily be understood that such a man as Douglass, thrown thus into stimulating daily intercourse with some of the brightest minds of his generation, all animated by a high and noble enthusiasm for liberty and humanity,—such men as Garrison and Phillips and Gay and Monroe and many others,—should have developed with remarkable rapidity those reserves of character and intellect which slavery had kept in repression. And yet, while aware of his wonderful talent for oratory, he never for a moment let this knowledge turn his head or obscure the consciousness that he had brought with him out of slavery of some of the disabilities of that status. Naturally, his expanding intelligence sought a wider range of expression; and his simple narrative of the wrongs of slavery gave way sometimes to a discussion of its philosophy. His abolitionist friends would have preferred him to stick a little more closely to the old line,—to furnish the experience while they provided the argument. But the strong will that slavery had not been able to break was not always amenable to politic suggestion. Douglass's style and vocabulary and logic improved so rapidly that people began to question his having been a slave. His appearance, speech, and manner differed so little in material particulars from those of his excellent exemplars that many people were sceptical of his antecedents. Douglass had, since his escape from slavery, carefully kept silent about the place he came from and his master's name and the manner of his escape, for the very good reason that their revelation would have informed his master of his whereabouts and rendered his freedom precarious; for the fugitive slave law was in force, and only here and there could local public sentiment have prevented its operation. Confronted with the probability of losing his usefulness, as the "awful example," Douglass took the bold step of publishing in the spring of 1845 the narrative of his experience as a slave, giving names of people and places, and dates as nearly as he could recall them. His abolitionist friends doubted the expediency of this step; and Wendell Phillips advised him to throw the manuscript into the fire, declaring that the government of Massachusetts had neither the power nor the will to protect him from the consequences of his daring.

The pamphlet was widely read. It was written in a style of graphic simplicity, and was such an *exposé* of slavery as exasperated its jealous supporters and beneficiaries. Douglass soon had excellent reasons to fear that he would be recaptured by force or guile and returned to slavery or a worse fate. The prospect was not an alluring one; and hence, to avoid an involuntary visit to the scenes of his childhood, he sought liberty beyond the sea, where men of his color have always enjoyed a larger freedom than in their native land.

In 1845 Douglass set sail for England on board the *Cambria*, of the Cunard Line, accompanied by James N. Buffum, a prominent abolitionist of Lynn, Massachusetts. On the same steamer were the Hutchinson family, who lent their sweet songs to the anti-slavery crusade. Douglass's color rendered him ineligible for cabin passage, and he was relegated to the steerage. Nevertheless, he became quite the lion of the vessel, made the steerage fashionable, was given the freedom of the ship, and invited to lecture on slavery. This he did to the satisfaction of all the passengers except a few young men from New Orleans and Georgia, who, true to the instincts of their caste, made his strictures on the South a personal matter, and threatened to throw him overboard. Their zeal was diminished by an order of the captain to put them in irons. They sulked in their cabins, however, and rushed into print when they reached Liverpool, thus giving Douglass the very introduction he needed to the British public, which was promptly informed, by himself and others, of the true facts in regard to the steamer speech and the speaker.

VI.

The two years Douglass spent in Great Britain upon this visit were active and fruitful ones, and did much to bring him to that full measure of development scarcely possible for him in slave-ridden America. For while the English government had fostered slavery prior to the Revolution, and had only a few years before Douglass's visit abolished it in its own colonies, this wretched system had never fastened its clutches upon the home islands. Slaves had been brought to England, it is true, and carried away; but, when the right to remove them was questioned in court, Lord Chief Justice Mansfield, with an abundance of argument and precedent to support a position similar to that of Justice Taney in the Dred Scott case, had taken the contrary view, and declared that the air of England was free, and the slave who breathed it but once ceased thereby to be a slave. History and humanity have delivered their verdict on these two decisions, and time is not likely to disturb it.

A few days after landing at Liverpool, Douglass went to Ireland, where the agitation for the repeal of the union between Great Britain and Ireland was in full swing, under the leadership of Daniel O'Connell, the great Irish orator. O'Connell had denounced slavery in words of burning eloquence. The Garrisonian abolitionists advocated the separation of the free and slave States as the only means of securing some part of the United States to freedom. The American and Irish disunionists were united by a strong bond of sympathy. Douglass was soon referred to as "the black O'Connell," and lectured on slavery and on temperance to large and enthusiastic audiences. He was introduced to O'Connell, and exchanged compliments with him. A public breakfast was given him at Cork, and a soirée by Father Matthew, the eminent leader of the great temperance crusade which at that time shared with the repeal agitation the public interest of Ireland. A reception to Douglass and his friend

Buffum was held in St. Patrick's Temperance Hall, where they were greeted with a special song of welcome, written for the occasion. On January 6, 1846, a public breakfast was given Douglass at Belfast, at which the local branch of the British and Foreign Anti-slavery Society presented him with a Bible bound in gold.

After four months in Ireland, where he delivered more than fifty lectures, Douglass and his friend Buffum left Ireland, on January 10, 1846, for Scotland, where another important reform was in progress. It was an epoch of rebellion against the established order of things. The spirit of revolt was in the air. The disruption movement in the Established Church of Scotland, led by the famous Dr. Chalmers, had culminated in 1843 in the withdrawal of four hundred and seventy ministers, who gave up the shelter and security of the Establishment for the principle that a congregation should choose its own pastor, and organized themselves into the Free Protesting Church, commonly called the Free Kirk. An appeal had been issued to the Presbyterian churches of the world for aid to establish a sustentation fund for the use of the new church. Among the contributions from the United States was one from a Presbyterian church in Charleston, South Carolina. Just before this contribution arrived a South Carolina judge had condemned a Northern man to death for aiding the escape of a female slave. This incident had aroused horror and indignation throughout Great Britain. Lord Brougham had commented on it in the House of Lords, and Lord Chief Justice Denham had characterized it "in the name of all the judges of England" as a "horrible iniquity." O'Connell had rejected profferred contributions from the Southern States, and an effort was made in Scotland to have the South Carolina money sent back. The attempt failed ultimately; but the agitation on the subject was for a time very fierce, and gave Douglass and his friends the opportunity to strike many telling blows at slavery. He had never minced his words in the United States, and he now handled without gloves the government whose laws had driven him from its borders.

From Scotland Douglass went to England, where he found still another great reform movement nearing a triumphant conclusion. The Anti-corn Law League, after many years of labor, under the leadership of Richard Cobden and John Bright, for the abolition of the protective tariff on wheat and other kinds of grain for food, had brought its agitation to a successful issue; and on June 26, 1846, the Corn Laws were repealed. The generous enthusiasm for reform of one kind or another that pervaded the British Islands gave ready sympathy and support to the abolitionists in their mission. The abolition of slavery in the colonies had been decreed by Parliament in 1833, but the old leaders in that reform had not lost their zeal for liberty. George Thompson, who with Clarkson and Wilberforce had led the British abolitionists, invited Garrison over to help reorganize the anti-slavery sentiment of Great Britain against American slavery; and in August, 1846, Garrison went to England, in that year evidently a paradise of reformers.

During the week beginning May 17, 1846, Douglass addressed respectively the annual meeting of the British and Foreign Anti-slavery Society, a peace convention, a suffrage extension meeting, and a temperance convention, and spoke also at a reception where efforts were made to induce him to remain in England, and money subscribed to bring over his family. As will be seen hereafter, he chose the alternative of returning to the United States.

On August 7, 1846, Douglass addressed the World's Temperance Convention, held at Covent Garden Theatre, London. There were many speakers, and the time allotted to each was brief; but Douglass never lost an opportunity to attack slavery, and he did so on this occasion over the shoulder of temperance. He stated that he was not a delegate to the convention, because those whom he might have represented were placed beyond the pale of American temperance societies either by slavery or by an inveterate prejudice against their color. He referred to the mobbing of a procession of colored temperance societies in Philadelphia several years before, the burning of one of their churches, and the wrecking of their best temperance hall. These remarks brought out loud protests and calls for order from the American delegates present, who manifested the usual American sensitiveness to criticism, especially on the subject of slavery; but the house sustained Douglass, and demanded that he go on. Douglass was denounced for this in a letter to the New York papers by Rev. Dr. Cox, one of the American delegates. Douglass's reply to this letter gave him the better of the controversy. He sometimes expressed the belief, founded on long experience, that doctors of divinity were, as a rule, among the most ardent supporters of slavery. Dr. Cox, who seems at least to have met the description, was also a delegate to the Evangelical Alliance, which met in London, August 19, 1846, with a membership of one thousand delegates from fifty different evangelical sects throughout the world. The question was raised in the convention whether or not fellowship should be held with slaveholders. Dr. Cox and the other Americans held that it should, and their views ultimately prevailed. Douglass made some telling speeches at Anti-slavery League meetings, in denunciation of the cowardice of the Alliance, and won a wide popularity.

Douglass remained in England two years. Not only did this visit give him a great opportunity to influence British public opinion against slavery, but the material benefits to himself were inestimable. He had left the United States a slave before the law, denied every civil right and every social privilege, literally a man without a country, and forced to cross the Atlantic among the cattle in the steerage of the steamboat. During his sojourn in Great Britain an English lady, Mrs. Ellen Richardson, of Newcastle, had raised seven hundred and fifty dollars, which was paid over to Hugh Auld, of Maryland, to secure Douglass's legal manumission; and, not content with this generous work, the same large-hearted lady had raised by subscription about two thousand five hundred dollars, which Douglass carried back to the United States as a free gift, and used to start his newspaper. He had met in Europe, as he said in a farewell speech, men quite as white as he had ever seen in the United States and of quite as noble exterior, and had seen in their faces no scorn of his complexion. He had travelled over the four kingdoms, and had encountered no sign of disrespect. He had been lionized in London, had spoken every night of his last month there, and had declined as many more invitations. He had shaken hands with the venerable Clarkson, and had breakfasted with the philosopher Combe, the author of *The Constitution of Man*. He had won the friendship of John Bright, had broken bread with Sir John Bowring, had been introduced to Lord Brougham, the brilliant leader of the Liberal party, and had listened to his wonderful eloquence. He had met Douglas Jerrold, the famous wit, and had been entertained by the poet William Howitt, who made a farewell speech in his honor. Everywhere he had denounced slavery, everywhere hospitable doors had opened wide to receive him, everywhere he had made friends for himself and his cause. A slave and an outcast at home, he had been made to feel himself a gentleman, had been the companion of great men and good women. Urged to remain in this land of freedom, and offered aid to establish himself in life there, his heart bled for his less fortunate brethren in captivity; and, with the God-speed of his English friends ringing in his ears, he went back to America,—to scorn, to obloquy, to ostracism, but after all to the work to which he had been ordained, and which he was so well qualified to perform.

VII.

Douglass landed April 20, 1847. He returned to the United States with the intention of publishing the newspaper for which his English friends had so kindly furnished the means; but his plan meeting with opposition from his abolitionist friends, who thought the platform offered him a better field for usefulness, he deferred the enterprise until near the end of the year. In the mean time he plunged again into the thick of the anti-slavery agitation. We find him lecturing in May in the Broadway Tabernacle, New York, and writing letters to the anti-slavery papers. In June he was elected president of the New England Anti-slavery Convention. In August and September he went on a lecturing tour with Garrison and others through Pennsylvania and Ohio. On this tour the party attended the commencement exercises of Oberlin College, famous for its anti-slavery principles and practice, and spoke to immense meetings at various places in Ohio and New York. Their cause was growing in popular favor; and, in places where formerly they had spoken out of doors because of the difficulty of securing a place of meeting, they were now compelled to speak in the open air, because the churches and halls would not contain their audiences.

On December 3, 1847, the first number of the *North Star* appeared. Douglass's abolitionist friends had not yet become reconciled to this project, and his persistence in it resulted in a temporary coldness between them. They very naturally expected him to be guided by their advice. They had found him on the wharf at New Bedford, and given him his chance in life; and they may easily be pardoned for finding it presumptuous in him to disregard their advice and adopt a new line of conduct without consulting them. Mr. Garrison wrote in a letter to his wife from Cleveland, "It will also greatly surprise our friends in Boston to hear that in regard to his prospect of establishing a paper here, to be called the *North Star*, he never opened his lips to me on the subject nor asked my advice in any particular whatever." But Samuel May Jr., in a letter written to one of Douglass's English friends, in which he mentions this charge of Garrison, adds, "It is only common justice to Frederick Douglass to inform you that this is a mistake; that, on the contrary, he did speak to Mr. Garrison about it, just before he was taken ill at Cleveland." The probability is that Douglass had his mind made up, and did not seek advice, and that Mr. Garrison did not attach much importance to any casual remark Douglass may have made upon the subject. In a foot-note to the *Life and Times of Garrison* it is stated:—

"This enterprise was not regarded with favor by the leading abolitionists, who knew only too well the precarious support which a fifth anti-slavery paper, edited by a colored man, must have, and who appreciated to the full Douglass's unrivalled powers as a lecturer in the field. . . . As anticipated, it nearly proved the ruin of its projector; but by extraordinary exertions it was kept alive, not, however, on the platform of Garrisonian abolitionism. The necessary support could only be secured by a change of principles in accordance with Mr. Douglass's immediate (political abolition) environment."

Douglass's own statement does not differ very widely from this, except that he does not admit the mercenary motive for his change of principles. It was in deference, however, to the feelings of his former associates that the *North Star* was established at Rochester instead of in the East, where the field for anti-slavery papers was already fully occupied. In Rochester, then as now the centre of a thrifty, liberal, and progressive population, Douglass gradually won the sympathy and support which such an enterprise demanded.

The *North Star,* in size, typography, and interest, compared favorably with the other weeklies of the day, and lived for seventeen years. It had, however, its "ups and downs." At one time the editor had mortgaged his house to pay the running expenses; but friends came to his aid, his debts were paid, and the circulation of the paper doubled. In *My Bondage and My Freedom* Douglass gives the names of numerous persons who helped him in these earlier years of editorial effort, among whom were a dozen of the most distinguished public men of his day. After the *North Star* had been in existence several years, its name was changed to *Frederick Douglass's Paper*, to give it a more distinctive designation, the newspaper firmament already scintillating with many other "Stars."

In later years Douglass speaks of this newspaper enterprise as one of the wisest things he ever undertook. To paraphrase Lord Bacon's famous maxim, much reading of life and of books had made him a full man, and much speaking had made him a ready man. The attempt to put facts and arguments into literary form tended to make him more logical in reasoning and more exact in statement. One of the effects of Douglass's editorial responsibility and the influences brought to bear upon him by reason of it, was a change in his political views. Until he began the publication of the *North Star* and for several years thereafter, he was, with the rest of the Garrisonians, a pronounced disunionist. He held to the Garrisonian doctrine that the pro-slavery Constitution of the United States was a "league with death and a covenant with hell," maintained that anti-slavery men should not vote under it, and advocated the separation of the free States as the only means of preventing the utter extinction of freedom by the ever-advancing encroachments of the slave power. In Rochester he found himself in the region where the Liberty party, under the leadership of James G. Birney, Salmon P. Chase, Gerrit Smith, and others, had its largest support. The Liberty party maintained that slavery could be fought best with political weapons, that by the power of the ballot slavery could be confined strictly within its constitutional limits and prevented from invading new territory, and that it could be extinguished by the respective States whenever the growth of public opinion demanded it. One wing of the party took the more extreme ground that slavery was contrary to the true intent and meaning of the Constitution, and demanded that the country should return to the principles of liberty upon which it was founded. Though the more radical abolitionists were for a time bitterly opposed to these views, yet the Liberty party was the natural outgrowth of the abolition agitation. Garrison and Phillips and Douglass and the rest had planted, Birney and

Gerrit Smith and Chase and the rest watered, and the Union party, led by the great emancipator, garnered the grain after a bloody harvest.

Several influences must have co-operated to modify Douglass's political views. The moral support and occasional financial aid given his paper by members of the Liberty party undoubtedly predisposed him favorably to their opinions. His retirement as agent of the Anti-slavery Society and the coolness resulting therefrom had taken him out of the close personal contact with those fervent spirits who had led the van in the struggle for liberty. Their zeal had been more disinterested, perhaps, than Douglass's own; for, after all, they had no personal stake in the outcome, while to Douglass and his people the abolition of slavery was a matter of life and death. Serene in the high altitude of their convictions, the Garrisonians would accept no half-way measures, would compromise no principles, and, if their right arm offended them, would cut it off with sublime fortitude and cast it into the fire. They wanted a free country, where the fleeing victim of slavery could find a refuge. Douglass perceived the immense advantage these swarming millions would gain through being free in the States where they already were. He had always been minded to do the best thing possible. When a slave, he had postponed his escape until it seemed entirely feasible. When denied cabin passage on steamboats, he had gone in the steerage or on deck. When he had been refused accommodation in a hotel, he had sought it under any humble roof that offered. It would have been a fine thing in the abstract to refuse the half-loaf, but in that event we should have had no Frederick Douglass. It was this very vein of prudence, keeping always in view the object to be attained, and in a broad, non-Jesuitical sense subordinating the means to the end, that enabled Douglass to prolong his usefulness a generation after the abolition of slavery. Douglass in his *Life and Times* states his own case as follows:—

"After a time, a careful reconsideration of the subject convinced me that there was no necessity for dissolving the union between the Northern and Southern States; that to seek this dissolution was no part of my duty as an abolitionist; that to abstain from voting was to refuse to exercise a legitimate and powerful means for abolishing slavery; and that the Constitution of the United States not only contained no guarantees in favor of slavery, but, on the contrary, was in its letter and spirit an anti-slavery instrument, demanding the abolition of slavery as a condition of its own existence, as the supreme law of the land."

This opinion was not exactly the opinion of the majority of the Liberty party, which did not question the constitutionality of slavery in the slave States. Neither was it the opinion of the Supreme Court, which in the Dred Scott case held that the Constitution guaranteed not only the right to hold slaves, but to hold them in free States. Nevertheless, entertaining the views he did, Douglass was able to support the measures which sought to oppose slavery through political action. In August, 1848, while his Garrisonian views were as yet unchanged, he had been present as a spectator at the Free Soil Convention at Buffalo. In his *Life and Times* he says of this gathering: "This Buffalo Convention of Free Soilers, however low their standard, did lay the foundation of a grand superstructure. It was a powerful link in the chain of events by which the slave system has been abolished, the slave emancipated, and the country saved from dismemberment." In 1851 Douglass announced that his sympathies were with the voting abolitionists, and thenceforth he supported by voice and pen Hale, Fremont, and Lincoln, the successive candidates of the new party.

Douglass's political defection very much intensified the feeling against him among his former coadjutors. The Garrisonians, with their usual plain speaking, did not hesitate to say what they thought of Douglass. Their three papers, the *Liberator*, the *Standard*, and the *Freeman*, assailed Douglass fiercely, and charged him with treachery, inconsistency, ingratitude, and all the other crimes so easily imputed to one who changes his opinions. Garrison and Phillips and others of his former associates denounced him as a deserter, and attributed his change of heart to mercenary motives. Douglass seems to have borne himself with rare dignity and moderation in this trying period. He realized perfectly well that he was on the defensive, and that the burden devolved upon him to justify his change of front. This he seems to have attempted vigorously, but by argument rather than invective. Even during the height of the indignation against him Douglass disclaimed any desire to antagonize his former associates. He simply realized that there was more than one way to fight slavery,—which knew a dozen ways to maintain itself,—and had concluded to select the one that seemed most practical. He was quite willing that his former friends should go their own way. "No personal assaults," he wrote to George Thompson, the English abolitionist, who wrote to him for an explanation of the charges made against him, "shall ever lead me to forget that some, who in America have often made me the subject of personal abuse, are in their own way earnestly working for the abolition of slavery."

In later years, when political action had resulted in abolition, some of these harsh judgments were modified, and Douglass and his earlier friends met in peace and harmony. The debt he owed to William Lloyd Garrison he ever delighted to acknowledge. His speech on the death of Garrison breathes in every word the love and honor in which he held him. In one of the last chapters of his *Life and Times* he makes a sweeping acknowledgment of his obligations to the men and women who rendered his career possible.

"It was my good fortune," he writes, "to get out of slavery at the right time, to be speedily brought in contact with that circle of highly cultivated men and women, banded together for the overthrow of slavery, of which William Lloyd Garrison was the acknowledged leader. To these friends, earnest, courageous, inflexible, ready to own me as a man and a brother, against all the scorn, contempt, and derision of a slavery-polluted atmosphere, I owe my success in life."

VIII.

Events moved rapidly in the decade preceding the war. In 1850 the new Fugitive Slave Law brought discouragement to the hearts of the friends of liberty. Douglass's utterances during this period breathed the fiery indignation which he felt when the slave-driver's whip was heard cracking over the free States, and all citizens were ordered to aid in the enforcement of this inhuman statute when called upon. This law really defeated its own purpose. There were thousands of conservative Northern men, who, recognizing the constitutional guarantees of slavery and the difficulty of abolishing it unless the South should take the initiative, were content that it should be preserved intact so long as it remained a local institution. But when the attempt was made to make the North wash the South's dirty linen, and transform every man in the Northern States into a slave-catcher, it wrought a revulsion of feeling that aroused widespread sympathy for the slave and strengthened the cause of freedom amazingly. Thousands of escaped slaves were living in Northern communities. Some of them had acquired homes, had educated their children, and in some States had become citizens and voters. Already social pariahs, restricted generally to menial labor, bearing the burdens of poverty and prejudice, they now had thrust before them the spectre of the kidnapper, the slave-catcher with his affidavit, and the United States [Supreme] Court, which was made by this law the subservient tool of tyranny. This law gave Douglass and the other abolitionists a new text. It was a set-back to their cause; but they were not entirely disheartened, for they saw in it the desperate expedients by which it was sought to bolster up an institution already doomed by the advancing tide of civilization.

The loss of slaves had become a serious drain upon the border States. The number of refugees settled in the North was, of course, largely a matter of estimate. Runaway slaves were not apt to advertise their status, but rather to conceal it, so that most estimates were more likely to be under than over the truth. Henry Wilson places the number in the free States at twenty thousand. There were in Boston in 1850, according to a public statement of Theodore Parker, from four to six hundred; and in other New England towns, notably New Bedford, the number was large. Other estimates place the figures much higher. Mr. Siebert, in his *Underground Railroad*, after a careful calculation from the best obtainable data, puts the number of fugitives aided in Ohio alone at forty thousand in the thirty years preceding 1860, and in the same period nine thousand in the city of Philadelphia alone, which was one of the principal stations of the underground railroad and the home of William Still, whose elaborate work on the *Underground Railroad* gives the details of many thrilling escapes.

In the work of assisting runaway slaves Douglass found congenial employment. It was exciting and dangerous, but inspiring and soul-satisfying. He kept a room in his house always ready for fugitives, having with him as many as eleven at a time. He would keep them over night, pay their fare on the train for Canada, and give them half a dollar extra. And Canada, to her eternal honor be it said, received these assisted emigrants, with their fifty cents apiece, of alien race, debauched by slavery, gave them welcome and protection, refused to enter into diplomatic relations for their rendition to bondage, and spoke well of them as men and citizens when Henry Clay and the other slave [pro-slavery] leaders denounced them as the most worthless of their class. The example of Canada may be commended to those persons in the United States, of little faith, who, because in thirty years the emancipated race have not equalled the white man in achievement, are fearful lest nothing good can be expected of them.

In the stirring years of the early fifties Douglass led a busy life. He had each week to fill the columns of his paper and raise the money to pay its expenses. Add to this his platform work and the underground railroad work, which consisted not only in personal aid to the fugitives, but in raising money to pay their expenses, and his time was very adequately employed. In every anti-slavery meeting his face was welcome, and his position as a representative of his own peculiar people was daily strengthened. When *Uncle Tom's Cabin,* in 1852, set the world on fire over the wrongs of the slave,—or rather the wrongs of slavery, for that wonderful book did not portray the negro as the only sufferer from this hoary iniquity,—Mrs. Stowe, in her new capacity as a champion of liberty, conceived the plan of raising a fund for the benefit of the colored race, and in 1853 invited Douglass to visit her at Andover, Massachusetts, where she consulted with him in reference to the establishment of an industrial institute or trades school for colored youth, with a view to improving their condition in the free States. Douglass approved heartily of this plan, and through his paper made himself its sponsor. When, later on, Mrs. Stowe abandoned the project, Douglass was made the subject of some criticism, though he was not at all to blame for Mrs. Stowe's altered plans. In our own time the value of such institutions has been widely recognized, and the success of those at Hampton and Tuskegee has stimulated anew the interest in industrial education as one important factor in the elevation of the colored race.

In the years from 1853 to 1860 the slave power, inspired with divine madness, rushed headlong toward its doom. The arbitrary enforcement of the Fugitive Slave Act; the struggle between freedom and slavery in Kansas; the Dred Scott decision, by which a learned and subtle judge, who had it within his power to enlarge the boundaries of human liberty and cover his own name with glory, deliberately and laboriously summarized and dignified with the sanction of a court of last resort all the most odious prejudices that had restricted the opportunities of the colored people; the repeal of the Missouri Compromise; the John Brown raid; the [1855] assault on [Massachusetts antislavery U.S. Senator] Charles Sumner,—each of these incidents has been, in itself, the subject of more than one volume. Of these events the Dred Scott decision was the most disheartening. Douglass was not proof against the universal gloom, and began to feel that there was little hope of the peaceful solution of the question of slavery. It was in one of his darker moments that old Sojourner Truth, whose face appeared in so many anti-slavery gatherings, put her famous question, which breathed a sublime and childlike faith in God, even when his hand seemed heaviest on her people: "Frederick," she asked, "is God dead?" The orator paused impressively, and then thundered in a voice that thrilled his audience with prophetic intimations, "No, God is not dead; and therefore it is that slavery must end in blood!"

During this period John Brown stamped his name indelibly upon American history. It was almost inevitable that a man of the views, activities, and prominence of Douglass should become acquainted with John Brown. Their first meeting, however, was in 1847, more than ten years before the tragic episode at Harper's Ferry. At that time Brown was a merchant at Springfield, Massachusetts, whither Douglass was invited to visit him. In his *Life and Times* he describes Brown as a prosperous merchant, who in his home lived with the utmost abstemiousness, in order that he might save money for the great scheme he was already revolving. "His wife believed in him, and his children observed him with reverence. His arguments seemed to convince all, his appeals touched all, and his will impressed all. Certainly, I never felt myself in the presence of stronger religious influence than while in this man's house." There in his own home, where Douglass stayed as his guest, Brown outlined a plan which in substantially the same form he held dear to his heart for a decade longer. This plan, briefly stated, was to establish camps at certain easily defended points in the Allegheny Mountains; to send emissaries down to the plantations in the lowlands, starting in Virginia, and draw off the slaves to these mountain fastnesses; to maintain bands of them there, if possible, as a constant menace to slavery and an example of freedom; or, if that were impracticable, to lead them to Canada from time to time by the most available routes. Wild as this plan may seem in the light of the desperate game subsequently played by slavery, it did not at the time seem impracticable to such level-headed men as Theodore Parker and Thomas Wentworth Higginson.

Douglass's views were very much colored by his association with Brown; but, with his usual prudence and foresight, he pointed out the difficulties of this plan. From the time of their first meeting the relations of the two men were friendly and confidential. Captain Brown had his scheme ever in mind, and succeeded in convincing Douglass and others that it would subserve a useful purpose,—that, even if it resulted in failure, it would stir the conscience of the nation to a juster appreciation of the iniquity of slavery.

The Kansas troubles, however, turned Brown's energies for a time into a different channel. After Kansas had been secured to freedom, he returned with renewed ardor to his old project. He stayed for three weeks at Douglass's house at Rochester, and while there carried on an extensive correspondence with sympathizers and supporters, and thoroughly demonstrated to all with whom he conversed that he was a man of one all-absorbing idea.

In 1859, very shortly before the raid at Harper's Ferry, Douglass met Brown by appointment, in an abandoned stone quarry near Chambersburg, Pennsylvania. John Brown was already an outlaw, with a price upon his head; for a traitor had betrayed his plan the year before, and he had for this reason deferred its execution for a year. The meeting was surrounded by all the mystery and conducted with all the precautions befitting a meeting of conspirators. Brown had changed the details of his former plan, and told Douglass of his determination to take Harper's Ferry. Douglass opposed the measure vehemently, pointing out its certain and disastrous failure. Brown met each argument with another, and was not to be swayed from his purpose. They spent more than a day together discussing the details of the movement. When the more practical Douglass declined to take part in Brown's attempt, the old man threw his arms around his swarthy friend, in a manner typical of his friendship for the dark race, and said: "Come with me, Douglass, I will defend you with my life. I want you for a special purpose. When I strike, the bees will begin to swarm, and I shall want you to help hive them." But Douglass would not be persuaded. His abandonment of his old friend on the eve of a desperate enterprise was criticised by some, who, as Douglass says, "kept even farther from this brave and heroic man than I did." John Brown went forth to meet a felon's fate and wear a martyr's crown: Douglass lived to fight the battles of his race for years to come. There was room for both, and each played the part for which he was best adapted. It would have strengthened the cause of liberty very little for Douglass to die with Brown.

It is quite likely, however, that he narrowly escaped Brown's fate. When the raid at Harper's Ferry had roused the country, Douglass, with other leading Northern men, was indicted in Virginia for complicity in the affair. Brown's correspondence had fallen into the hands of the Virginia authorities, and certain letters seemed to implicate Douglass. A trial in Virginia meant almost certain death. Governor Wise, of Virginia, would have hung him with cheerful alacrity, and publicly expressed his desire to do so. Douglass, with timely warning that extradition papers had been issued for his arrest, escaped to Canada. He had previously planned a second visit to England, and the John Brown affair had delayed his departure by some days. He sailed from Quebec, November 12, 1859.

After a most uncomfortable winter voyage of fourteen days Douglass found himself again in England, an object of marked interest and in very great demand as a speaker. Six months he spent on the hospitable shores of Great Britain, lecturing on John Brown, on slavery and other subjects, and renewing the friendships of former years. Being informed of the death of his youngest daughter, he cut short his visit, which he had meant to extend to France, and returned to the United States. So rapid had been the course of events since his departure that the excitement over the John Brown raid had subsided. The first Lincoln campaign was in active progress; and the whole country quivered with vague anticipation of the impending crisis which was to end the conflict of irreconcilable principles, and sweep slavery out of the path of civilization and progress. Douglass plunged into the campaign with his accustomed zeal, and did what he could to promote the triumph of the Republican party. Lincoln was elected, and in a few short months the country found itself in the midst of war. God was not dead, and slavery was to end in blood.

IX.

Ever mindful of his people and seeking always to promote their welfare, Douglass was one of those who urged, in all his addresses at this period, the abolition of slavery and the arming of the negroes as the most effective means of crushing the rebellion. In 1862 he delivered a series of lectures in New England under the auspices of the recently formed Emancipation League, which contended for abolition as a military necessity.

The first or conditional emancipation proclamation was issued in September, 1862; and shortly afterward Douglass published a pamphlet for circulation in Great Britain, entitled *The Slave's Appeal to Great Britain,* in which he urged the English people to refuse recognition of the independence of the Confederate States. He always endeavored in his public utterances to remove the doubts and fears of those who were tempted to leave the negroes in slavery because of the difficulty of disposing of them after they became free. Douglass, with the simple, direct, primitive sense of justice that had always marked his mind, took the only true ground for the solution of the race problems of that or any other epoch,—that the situation should be met with equal and exact justice, and that his people should be allowed to do as they pleased with themselves, "subject only to the same great laws which apply to other men." He was a conspicuous figure at the meeting in Tremont Temple, Boston, on January 1, 1863, when the Emancipation Proclamation, hourly expected by an anxious gathering, finally flashed over the wires.

Douglass was among the first to suggest the employment of colored troops in the Union army. In spite of all assertions to the contrary, he foresaw in the war the end of slavery. He perceived that by the enlistment of colored men not only would the Northern arms be strengthened, but his people would win an opportunity to exercise one of the highest rights of freemen, and by valor on the field of battle to remove some of the stigma that slavery had placed upon them. He strove through every channel at his command to impress his views upon the country; and his efforts helped to swell the current of opinion which found expression, after several intermediate steps, in the enlistment of two colored regiments by Governor Andrew, the famous war governor of Massachusetts, a State foremost in all good works. When Mr. Lincoln had granted permission for the recruiting of these regiments, Douglass issued through his paper a stirring appeal, which was copied in the principal journals of the Union States, exhorting his people to rally to this call, to seize this opportunity to strike a blow at slavery and win the gratitude of the country and the blessings of liberty for themselves and their posterity.

Douglass exerted himself personally in procuring enlistments, his two sons [his youngest and his oldest], Charles and Lewis, being [among] the first in New York to enlist; for the two Massachusetts regiments were recruited all over the North. Lewis H. Douglass, sergeant-major in the Fifty-fourth Massachusetts, was among the foremost on the ramparts at Fort Wagner. Both these sons of Douglass survived the war, and are now well known and respected citizens of Washington, D.C. The Fifty-fourth Massachusetts, under the gallant but ill-fated Colonel Shaw, won undying glory in the conflict; and the heroic deeds of the officers and men of this regiment are fittingly commemorated in the noble monument by St. Gaudens, recently erected on Boston Common, to stand as an inspiration of freedom and patriotism for the future and as testimony that a race which for generations had been deprived of arms and liberty could worthily bear the one and defend the other.

Douglass was instrumental in persuading the government to put colored soldiers on an equal footing with white soldiers, both as to pay and protection. In the course of these efforts he was invited to visit President Lincoln. He describes this memorable interview in detail in his *Life and Times*. The President welcomed him with outstretched hands, put him at once at his ease, and listened patiently and attentively to all that he had to say. Douglass maintained that colored soldiers should receive the same pay as white soldiers, should be protected and exchanged as prisoners, and should be rewarded, by promotion, for deeds of valor. The President suggested some of the difficulties to be overcome; but both he and Secretary of War Stanton, whom Douglass also visited, assured him that in the end his race should be justly treated. Stanton, before the close of the interview with him, promised Douglass a commission as assistant adjutant to General Lorenzo Thomas, then recruiting colored troops in the Mississippi Valley. But Stanton evidently changed his mind, since the commission, somewhat to Douglass's chagrin, never came to hand.

When McClellan had been relieved by Grant, and the new leader of the Union forces was fighting the stubbornly contested campaign of the Wilderness, President Lincoln again sent for Douglass, to confer with him with reference to bringing slaves in the rebel States within the Union lines, so that in the event of premature peace as many slaves as possible might be free. Douglass undertook, at the President's suggestion, to organize a band of colored scouts to go among the negroes and induce them to enter the Union lines. The plan was never carried out, owing to the rapid success of the Union arms; but the interview greatly impressed Douglass with the sincerity of the President's conviction against slavery and his desire to see the war result in its overthrow. What the colored race may have owed to the services, in such a quarter, of such an advocate as Douglass, brave, eloquent, high-principled, and an example to Lincoln of what the enslaved race was capable of, can only be imagined. That Lincoln was deeply impressed by these interviews is a matter of history.

Douglass supported vigorously the nomination of Lincoln for a second term, and was present at his [March 4] inauguration. And a few days later, while the inspired words of the inaugural address, long bracketed with the noblest of human utterances, were still ringing in his ears, he spoke at the meeting held in Rochester to mourn the death of the martyred President, and made one of his most eloquent and moving addresses. It was a time that wrung men's hearts, and none more than the strong-hearted man's whose race had found its liberty through him who lay dead at Washington, slain by the hand of an assassin whom slavery had spawned.

X.

With the fall of slavery and the emancipation of the colored race the heroic epoch of Douglass's career may be said to have closed. The text upon which he so long had preached had been expunged from the national bible; and he had been a one-text preacher, a one-theme orator. He felt the natural reaction which comes with relief from high mental or physical tension, and wondered, somewhat sadly, what he should do with himself, and how he should earn a living. The same considerations, in varying measure, applied to others of the anti-slavery reformers. Some, unable to escape the reforming habit, turned their attention to different social evils, real or imaginary. Others, sufficiently supplied with this world's goods for their moderate wants, withdrew from public life. Douglass was thinking of buying a farm and retiring to rural solitudes, when a new career opened up for him in the lyceum lecture field. The North was favorably disposed toward colored men. They had acquitted themselves well during the war, and had shown becoming gratitude to their deliverers. The once despised abolitionists were now popular heroes. Douglass's checkered past seemed all the more romantic in the light of the brighter present, like a novel with a pleasant ending; and those who had hung thrillingly upon his words when he denounced slavery now listened with interest to what he had to say upon other topics. He spoke sometimes on Woman Suffrage, of which he was always a consistent advocate. His most popular lecture was one on "Self-made Men." Another on "Ethnology," in which he sought a scientific basis for his claim for the negro's equality with the white man, was not so popular—with white people. The wave of enthusiasm which had swept the enfranchised slaves into what seemed at that time the safe harbor of constitutional right was not, after all, based on abstract doctrines of equality of intellect, but on an inspiring sense of justice (long dormant under the influence of slavery, but thoroughly awakened under the moral stress of the war), which conceded to every man the right of a voice in his own government and the right to an equal opportunity in life to develop such powers as he possessed, however great or small these might be.

But Douglass's work in direct behalf of his race was not yet entirely done. In fact, he realized very distinctly the vast amount of work that would be necessary to lift his people up to the level of their enlarged opportunities; and, as may be gathered from some of his published utterances, he foresaw that the process would be a long one, and that their friends might weary sometimes of waiting, and that there would be reactions toward slavery which would rob emancipation of much of its value. It was the very imminence of such backward steps, in the shape of various restrictive and oppressive laws promptly enacted by the old slave States under President Johnson's administration,[1] that led Douglass to urge the enfranchisement of the freedmen. He maintained that in a free country there could be no safe or logical middle ground between the status of freeman and that of serf. There has been much criticism because the negro, it is said, acquired the ballot prematurely. There seemed imperative reasons, besides that of political expediency, for putting the ballot in his hands. Recent events have demonstrated that this necessity is as great now as then. The assumption that negroes—under which generalization are included all men of color, regardless of that sympathy to which kinship at least should entitle many of them—are unfit to have a voice in government is met by the words of Lincoln, which have all the weight of a political axiom: "No man can be safely trusted to govern other men without their consent." The contention that a class who constitute half the population of a State shall be entirely unrepresented in its councils, because, forsooth, their will there

---

[1] Editor's Note to Dover Edition. Vice-President Andrew Johnson (1808–1875) of Tennessee became President when Abraham Lincoln was assassinated on April 15, 1865. He presided over the Reconstruction of the South until his inherited term ended in March 1869. In May 1868 President Johnson was acquitted of impeachment charges brought against him in the U.S. Senate.

expressed may affect the government of another class of the same general population, is as repugnant to justice and human rights as was the institution of slavery itself. Such a condition of affairs has not the melodramatic and soul-stirring incidents of chattel slavery, but its effects can be as far-reaching and as debasing. There has been some manifestation of its possible consequences in the recent outbreaks of lynching and other race oppression in the South. The practical disfranchisement of the colored people in several States, and the apparent acquiescence by the Supreme Court in the attempted annulment, by restrictive and oppressive laws, of the war amendments to the Constitution, have brought a foretaste of what might be expected should the spirit of the Dred Scott decision become again the paramount law of the land.

On February 7, 1866, Douglass acted as chief spokesman of a committee of leading colored men of the country, who called upon President Johnson to urge the importance of enfranchisement. Mr. Johnson, true to his Southern instincts, was coldly hostile to the proposition, recounted all the arguments against it, and refused the committee an opportunity to reply. The matter was not left with Mr. Johnson, however; and the committee turned its attention to the leading Republican statesmen, in whom they found more impressionable material. Under the leadership of Senators Sumner, Wilson, Wade, and others, the matter was fully argued in Congress, the Democratic party being in opposition, as always in national politics, to any measure enlarging the rights or liberties of the colored race.

In September, 1866, Douglass was elected a delegate from Rochester to the National Loyalists' Convention at Philadelphia, called to consider the momentous questions of government growing out of the war. While he had often attended anti-slavery conventions as the representative of a small class of abolitionists, his election to represent a large city in a national convention was so novel a departure from established usage as to provoke surprise and comment all over the country. On the way to Philadelphia he was waited upon by a committee of other delegates, who came to his seat on the train and urged upon him the impropriety of his taking a seat as a delegate. Douglass listened patiently, but declined to be moved by their arguments. He replied that he had been duly elected a delegate from Rochester, and he would represent that city in the convention. A procession of the members and friends of the convention was to take place on its opening day. Douglass was solemnly warned that, if he walked in the procession, he would probably be mobbed. But he had been mobbed before, more than once, and had lived through it; and he promptly presented himself at the place of assembly. His reception by his fellow-delegates was not cordial, and he seemed condemned to march alone in the procession, when Theodore Tilton, at that time editor of the *Independent,* paired off with him, and marched by his side through the streets of the Quaker City. The result was gratifying alike to Douglass and the friends of liberty and progress. He was cheered enthusiastically all along the line of march, and became as popular in the convention as he had hitherto been neglected.

A romantic incident of this march was a pleasant meeting, on the street, with a daughter of Mrs. Lucretia Auld, the mistress who had treated him kindly during his childhood on the Lloyd plantation. The Aulds had always taken an interest in Douglass's career,—he had, indeed, given the family a wide though not altogether enviable reputation in his books and lectures,—and this good lady had followed the procession for miles, that she might have the opportunity to speak to her grandfather's former slave and see him walk in the procession.

In the convention "the ever-ready and imperial Douglass," as Colonel Higginson describes him, spoke in behalf of his race. The convention, however, divided upon the question of negro suffrage, and adjourned without decisive action. But under President Grant's administration the Fourteenth Amendment was passed, and by the solemn sanction of the Constitution the ballot was conferred upon the black men upon the same terms as those upon which it was enjoyed by the whites.

XI.

It is perhaps fitting, before we take leave of Douglass, to give some estimate of the remarkable oratory which gave him his hold upon the past generation. For, while his labors as editor and in other directions were of great value to the cause of freedom, it is upon his genius as an orator that his fame must ultimately rest.

While Douglass's color put him in a class by himself among great orators, and although his slave past threw around him an element of romance that added charm to his eloquence, these were mere incidental elements of distinction. The North was full of fugitive slaves, and more than one had passionately proclaimed his wrongs. There were several colored orators who stood high in the councils of the abolitionists and did good service for the cause of humanity.

Douglass possessed, in large measure, the physical equipment most impressive in an orator. He was a man of magnificent figure, tall, strong, his head crowned with a mass of hair which made a striking element of his appearance. He had deep-set and flashing eyes, a firm, well-moulded chin, a countenance somewhat severe in repose, but capable of a wide range of expression. His voice was rich and melodious, and of great carrying power. One writer, who knew him in the early days of his connection with the abolitionists, says of him, in Johnson's *Sketches of Lynn*:—

"He was not then the polished orator he has since become, but even at that early date he gave promise of the grand part he was to play in the conflict which was to end in the destruction of the system that had so long cursed his race. . . . He was more than six feet in height; and his majestic form, as he rose to speak, straight as an arrow, muscular yet lithe and graceful, his flashing eye, and more than all his voice, that rivalled Webster's in its richness and in the depth and sonorousness of its cadences, made up such an ideal of an orator as the listeners never forgot. And they never forgot his burning words, his pathos, nor the rich play of his humor."

The poet William Howitt said of him on his departure from England in 1847, "He has appeared in this country before the most accomplished audiences, who were surprised, not only at his talent, but at his extraordinary information."

In Ireland he was introduced as "the black O'Connell,"—a high compliment; for O'Connell was at that time the idol of the Irish people. In Scotland they called him the "black Douglass [Douglas]," after his prototype in *The Lady of the Lake*, because of his fire and vigor. In Rochester he was called the "swarthy Ajax," from his indignant denunciation and defiance of the Fugitive Slave Law of 1850, which came like a flash of lightning to blast the hopes of the anti-slavery people.

Douglass possessed in unusual degree the faculty of swaying his audience, sometimes against their maturer judgment. There is something in the argument from first principles which, if presented with force and eloquence, never fails to appeal to those who are not blinded by self-interest or deep-seated prejudice. Douglass's argument was that of the Declaration of Independence,—"that *all* men are created equal; that they are endowed by their Creator with certain inalienable rights; that among these are life, liberty, and the pursuit of happiness. That, to secure these rights, governments are instituted among men, deriving their just powers from the *consent of the governed*." The writer may be pardoned for this quotation; for there are times when we seem to forget that now and here, no less than in ancient Rome, "eternal vigilance is the price of liberty." Douglass brushed aside all sophistries about Constitutional guarantees, and vested rights, and inferior races, and, having postulated the right of men to be free, maintained that negroes were men, and offered himself as a proof of his assertion,— an argument that few had the temerity to deny. If it were answered that he was only half a negro, he would reply that slavery made no such distinction, and as a still more irrefutable argument would point to his friend, Samuel R. Ward, who often accompanied him on the platform,—an eloquent and effective orator, of whom Wendell Phillips said that "he was so black that, if he would shut his eyes, one could not see him." It was difficult for an auditor to avoid assent to such arguments, presented with all the force and fire of genius, relieved by a ready wit, a contagious humor, and a tear-compelling power rarely excelled.

"As a speaker," says one of his contemporaries, "he has few equals. It is not declamation, but oratory, power of description. He watches the tide of discussion, and dashes into it at once with all the tact of the forum or the bar. He has art, argument, sarcasm, pathos,—all that first-rate men show in their master efforts."

His readiness was admirably illustrated in the running debate with Captain Rynders, a ward politician and gambler of New York, who led a gang of roughs with the intention of breaking up the meeting of the American Anti-slavery Society in New York City, May 7, 1850. The newspapers had announced the proposed meeting in language calculated to excite riot. Rynders packed the meeting with rowdies, and himself occupied a seat on the platform. Some remark by Mr. Garrison, the first speaker, provoked a demonstration of hostility. When this was finally quelled by a promise to permit one of the Rynders party to reply, Mr. Garrison finished his speech. He was followed by a prosy individual, who branded the negro as brother to the monkey. Douglass, perceiving that the speaker was wearying even his own friends, intervened at an opportune moment, captured the audience by a timely display of wit, and then improved the occasion by a long and effective speech. When Douglass offered himself as a refutation of the last speaker's argument, Rynders replied that Douglass was half white. Douglass thereupon greeted Rynders as his half-brother, and made this expression the catchword of his speech. When Rynders interrupted from time to time, he was silenced with a laugh. He appears to have been a somewhat philosophic scoundrel, with an appreciation of humor that permitted the meeting to proceed to an orderly close. Douglass's speech was the feature of the evening. "That gifted man," said Garrison, in whose *Life and Times* a graphic description of this famous meeting is given, "effectually put to shame his assailants by his wit and eloquence."

A speech delivered by Douglass at Concord, New

Hampshire, is thus described by another writer: "He gradually let out the outraged humanity that was laboring in him, in indignant and terrible speech. . . . There was great oratory in his speech, but more of dignity and earnestness than what we call eloquence. He was an insurgent slave, taking hold on the rights of speech, and charging on his tyrants the bondage of his race."

In Holland's biography of Douglass extracts are given from letters of distinguished contemporaries who knew the orator. Colonel T. W. Higginson writes thus: "I have hardly heard his equal, in grasp upon an audience, in dramatic presentation, in striking at the pith of an ethical question, and in single [signal] illustrations and examples." Another writes, in reference to the impromptu speech delivered at the meeting at Rochester on the death of Lincoln: "I have heard Webster and Clay in their best moments, Channing and Beecher in their highest inspirations. I never heard truer eloquence. I never saw profounder impression."

The published speeches of Douglass, of which examples may be found scattered throughout his various autobiographies, reveal something of the powers thus characterized, though, like other printed speeches, they lose by being put in type. But one can easily imagine their effect upon a sympathetic or receptive audience, when delivered with flashing eye and deep-toned resonant voice by a man whose complexion and past history gave him the highest right to describe and denounce the iniquities of slavery and contend for the rights of a race. In later years, when brighter days had dawned for his people, and age had dimmed the recollection of his sufferings and tempered his animosities, he became more charitable to his old enemies; but in the vigor of his manhood, with the memory of his wrongs and those of his race fresh upon him, he possessed that indispensable quality of the true reformer: he went straight to the root of the evil, and made no admissions and no compromises. Slavery for him was conceived in greed, born in sin, cradled in shame, and worthy of utter and relentless condemnation. He had the quality of directness and simplicity. When Collins would have turned the abolition influence to the support of a communistic scheme, Douglass opposed it vehemently. Slavery was the evil they were fighting, and their cause would be rendered still more unpopular if they ran after strange gods.

When Garrison pleaded for the rights of man, when Phillips with golden eloquence preached the doctrine of humanity and progress, men approved and applauded. When Parker painted the moral baseness of the times, men acquiesced shamefacedly. When Channing[1] preached the gospel of love, they wished the dream might become a reality. But, when Douglass told the story of his wrongs and those of his brethren in bondage, they felt that here indeed was slavery embodied, here was an argument for freedom that could not be gainsaid, that the race that could produce in slavery such a man as Frederick Douglass must surely be worthy of freedom.

What Douglass's platform utterances in later years lacked of the vehemence and fire of his earlier speeches, they made up in wisdom and mature judgment. There is a note of exultation in his speeches just after the war. Jehovah had triumphed, his people were free. He had seen the Red Sea of blood open and let them pass, and engulf the enemy who pursued them.

Among the most noteworthy of Douglass's later addresses were the oration at the unveiling of the Freedmen's Monument to Abraham Lincoln in Washington in 1876, which may be found in his *Life and Times*; the address on Decoration Day, New York, 1878; his eulogy on Wendell Phillips, printed in Austin's *Life and Times of Wendell Phillips*; and the speech on the death of Garrison, June, 1879. He lectured in the Parker Fraternity Course in Boston, delivered numerous addresses to gatherings of colored men, spoke at public dinners and woman suffrage meetings, and retained his hold upon the interest of the public down to the very day of his death.

---

[1] Editor's Note to Dover Edition: William Henry Channing (1810–1884), like his uncle William Ellery Channing (1780–1842), was an eloquent New England Unitarian minister who opposed slavery.

XII.

With the full enfranchisement of his people, Douglass entered upon what may be called the third epoch of his career, that of fruition. Not every worthy life receives its reward in this world; but Douglass, having fought the good fight, was now singled out, by virtue of his prominence, for various honors and emoluments at the hands of the public. He was urged by many friends to take up his residence in some Southern district and run for Congress; but from modesty or some doubt of his fitness— which one would think he need not have felt—and the consideration that his people needed an advocate at the North to keep alive there the friendship and zeal for liberty that had accomplished so much for his race, he did not adopt the suggestion.

In 1860 [1870] Douglass moved to Washington, and began [took over] the publication of the *New National Era*, a weekly paper devoted to the interests of the colored race. The venture did not receive the support hoped for; and the paper was turned over to Douglass's two [oldest] sons, Lewis and Frederick, and was finally abandoned [in 1874], Douglass having sunk about ten thousand dollars in the enterprise. Later newspapers for circulation among the colored people have proved more successful; and it ought to be a matter of interest that the race which thirty years ago could not support one publication, edited by its most prominent man, now maintains several hundred newspapers which make their appearance regularly.

In 1871 Douglass was elected president of the Freedman's Bank. This ill-starred venture was then apparently in the full tide of prosperity, and promised to be a great lever in the uplifting of the submerged race. Douglass, soon after his election as president, discovered the insolvency of the institution, and insisted that it be closed up. The negro was in the hands of his friends, and was destined to suffer for their mistakes as well as his own.

Other honors that fell to Douglass were less empty than the presidency of a bankrupt bank. In 1870 he was appointed by President Grant a member of the Santo Domingo Commission, the object of which was to arrange terms for the annexation of the mulatto republic to the Union. Some of the best friends of the colored race, among them Senator Sumner, opposed this step; but Douglass maintained that to receive Santo Domingo as a State would add to its strength and importance. The scheme ultimately fell through, whether for the good or ill of Santo Domingo can best be judged when the results of more recent annexation schemes [1898: Puerto Rico, Guam, the Philippines, Hawaii, and *de facto* Cuba] become apparent. Douglass went to Santo Domingo on an American man-of-war, in the company of three other commissioners. In his *Life and Times* he draws a pleasing contrast between some of his earlier experiences in travelling, and the terms of cordial intimacy upon which, as the representative of a nation which a few years before had denied him a passport, he was now received in the company of able and distinguished gentlemen.

On his return to the United States Douglass received from President Grant an appointment as member of the legislative council, or upper house of the legislature, of the District of Columbia, where he served for a short time, until other engagements demanded his resignation, [one of] his son[s] being appointed to fill out his term. To this appointment Douglass owed the title of "Honorable," subsequently applied to him.

In 1872 Douglass presided over and addressed a convention of colored men at New Orleans, and urged them to support President Grant for renomination. He was elected a presidential elector for New York, and on the meeting of the electoral college in Albany, after Grant's triumphant re-election, received a further mark of confidence and esteem in the appointment at the hands of his fellow-electors to carry the sealed vote to Washington. Douglass sought no personal reward for his services in this campaign, but to his influence was due the appointment of several of his friends to higher positions than had ever theretofore been held in this country by colored men.

When R. B. Hayes was nominated for President, Douglass again took the stump, and received as a reward the honorable and lucrative office of Marshal of the United States for the District of Columbia. This appointment was not agreeable to the white people of the District, whose sympathies were largely pro-slavery; and an effort was made to have its confirmation defeated in the Senate. The appointment was confirmed, however; and Douglass served his term of four years, in spite of numerous efforts to bring about his removal.

In 1879 the hard conditions under which the negroes in the South were compelled to live led to a movement to promote an exodus of the colored people to the North and West, in the search for better opportunities. The white people of the South, alarmed at the prospect of losing their labor, were glad to welcome Douglass when he went among them to oppose this movement, which he at that time considered detrimental to the true interests of the colored population.

Under the Garfield administration Douglass was appointed in May, 1881, recorder of deeds for the District of Columbia. He held this very lucrative office through the terms of Presidents Garfield and Arthur and until removed by President Cleveland in 1886, having served nearly a year after Cleveland's inauguration. In 1889 he was appointed by President Harrison as minister resident and consul-general to the Republic of Hayti, in which capacity he acted until 1891, when he resigned and returned permanently to Washington. The writer has heard him speak with enthusiasm of the substantial progress made by the Haytians in the arts of government and civilization, and with indignation of what he considered slanders against the island, due to ignorance or prejudice. When it was suggested to Douglass that the Haytians were given to revolution as a mode of expressing disapproval of their rulers, he replied that a four years' rebellion had been fought and two Presidents assassinated in the United States during a comparatively peaceful political period in Hayti. His last official connection with the Black Republic was at the World's Columbian Exposition at Chicago in 1893, where he acted as agent in charge of the Haytian Building and the very creditable exhibit therein contained. His stately figure, which age had not bowed, his strong dark face, and his head of thick white hair made him one of the conspicuous features of the Exposition; and many a visitor took advantage of the occasion to recall old acquaintance made in the stirring anti-slavery days.

In 1878 he revisited the Lloyd plantation in Maryland, where he had spent part of his youth, and an affecting meeting took place between him and Thomas Auld, whom he had once called master. Once in former years he had been sought out by the good lady who in his childhood had taught him to read. Nowhere more than in his own accounts of these meetings does the essentially affectionate and forgiving character of Douglass and his race become apparent, and one cannot refrain from thinking that a different state of affairs might prevail in the Southern States if other methods than those at present in vogue were used to regulate the relations between the two races and their various admixtures that make up the Southern population.

In June, 1879, a bronze bust of Douglass was erected in Sibley Hall of Rochester University as a tribute to one who had shed lustre on the city. In 1882 occurred the death of Douglass's first wife, whom he had married in New York immediately after his escape from slavery, and who had been his faithful companion through so many years of stress and struggle. In the same year his *Life and Times* was published. In 1884 he married Miss Helen Pitts, a white woman of culture and refinement. There was some criticism of this step by white people who did not approve of the admixture of the races, and by colored persons who thought their leader had slighted his own people when he overlooked the many worthy and accomplished women among them. But Douglass, to the extent that he noticed these strictures at all, declared that he had devoted his life to breaking down the color line, and that he did not know any more effectual way to accomplish it; that he was white by half his blood, and, as he had given most of his life to his mother's race, he claimed the right to dispose of the remnant as he saw fit.

The latter years of his life were spent at his beautiful home known as Cedar Hill, on Anacostia Heights, near Washington, amid all

"that which should accompany old age,
As honor, love, obedience, troops of friends."

He possessed strong and attractive social qualities, and his home formed a Mecca for the advanced and aspiring of his race. He was a skilful violinist, and derived great pleasure from the valuable instrument he possessed. A wholesome atmosphere always surrounded him. He had never used tobacco or strong liquors, and was clean of speech and pure in life.

He died at his home in Washington, February 20, 1895. He had been perfectly well during the day, and was supposed to be in excellent health. He had attended both the forenoon and afternoon sessions of the Women's National Council, then in session at Washington, and had been a conspicuous figure in the audience. On his return home, while speaking to his wife in the hallway of his house, he suddenly fell, and before assistance could be given he had passed away.

His death brought forth many expressions from the press of the land, reflecting the high esteem in which he had been held by the public for a generation. In various cities meetings were held, at which resolutions of sorrow and appreciation were passed, and delegations appointed to attend his funeral. In the United States Senate a resolution was offered reciting that in the person of the late Frederick Douglass death had borne away a most illustrious citizen, and permitting the body to lie in state in the rotunda of the Capitol on Sunday. The immediate consideration of the resolution was asked for. Mr. Gorman, of Maryland, the State which Douglass honored by his birth, objected; and the resolution went over.

Douglass's funeral took place on February 25, 1895, at the Metropolitan African Methodist Episcopal Church in Washington, and was the occasion of a greater outpouring of colored people than had taken place in Washington since the unveiling of the Lincoln emancipation statue in 1878. The body was taken from Cedar Hill to the church at half-past nine in the morning; and from that hour until noon thousands of persons, including many white people, passed in double file through the building and viewed the body, which was in charge of a guard of

honor composed of members of a colored camp of the Sons of
Veterans. The church was crowded when the services began,
and several thousands could not obtain admittance.
Delegations, one of them a hundred strong, were present from
a dozen cities. Among the numerous floral tributes was a magnificent shield of roses, orchids, and palms, sent by the Haytian
government through its minister. Another tribute was from the
son of his old master. Among the friends of the deceased present were Senators Sherman and Hoar, Justice Harlan of the
Supreme Court, Miss Susan B. Anthony, and Miss May Wright
Sewall, president of the Women's National Council. The temporary pall-bearers were ex-Senator B. K. Bruce and other
prominent colored men of Washington. The sermon was
preached by Rev. J. G. Jenifer. John E. Hutchinson, the last of
the famous Hutchinson family of abolition singers, who with his
sister accompanied Douglass on his first voyage to England,
sang two requiem solos, and told some touching stories of their
old-time friendship. The remains were removed to Douglass's
former home in Rochester, where he was buried with unusual
public honors.

In November, 1894, a movement was begun in Rochester,
under the leadership of J. W. Thompson, with a view to erect a
monument in memory of the colored soldiers and sailors who
had fallen during the Civil War. This project had the hearty support and assistance of Douglass; and upon his death the plan was
changed, and a monument to Douglass himself decided upon. A
contribution of one thousand dollars from the Haytian government and an appropriation of three thousand dollars from the
State of New York assured the success of the plan. September
15, 1898, was the date set for the unveiling of the monument;
but, owing to delay in the delivery of the statue, only a part of
the contemplated exercises took place. The monument, complete with the exception of the statue which was to surmount it,
was formally turned over to the city, the presentation speech
being made by Charles P. Lee of Rochester. A solo and chorus
composed for the occasion were sung, an original poem read by
T. Thomas Fortune, and addresses delivered by John C. Dancy
and John H. Smyth. Joseph H. Douglass, a talented grandson of

the orator, played a violin solo, and Miss Susan B. Anthony recalled some reminiscences of Douglass in the early anti-slavery days. In June, 1899, the bronze statue of Douglass, by Sidney W. Edwards, was installed with impressive ceremonies. The movement thus to perpetuate the memory of Douglass had taken rise among a little band of men of his own race, but the whole people of Rochester claimed the right to participate in doing honor to their distinguished fellow-citizen. The city assumed a holiday aspect. A parade of military and civic societies was held, and an appropriate programme rendered at the unveiling of the monument. Governor Roosevelt of New York[1] delivered an address; and the occasion took a memorable place in the annals of Rochester, of which city Douglass had said, "I shall always feel more at home there than anywhere else in this country."

In March, 1895, a few weeks after the death of Douglass, Theodore Tilton, his personal friend for many years, published in Paris, of which city he was then a resident, a volume of *Sonnets to the Memory of Frederick Douglass*, from which the following lines are quoted as the estimate of a contemporary and a fitting epilogue to this brief sketch of so long and full a life:—

> "I knew the noblest giants of my day,
>   And *he* was *of* them—strong amid the strong:
>   But gentle too: for though he suffered wrong,
> Yet the wrong-doer never heard him say,
> 'Thee also do I hate.' . . .
>   "A lover's lay—
>   No dirge—no doleful requiem song—
>   Is what I owe him; for I loved him long;
> As dearly as a younger brother may.

---

[1] Editor's Note to Dover Edition: Theodore Roosevelt (1858–1919), a Republican, was governor of New York State 1899–1901. In September 1901, when he was U.S. Vice-President, he became President when William McKinley was assassinated. Roosevelt was elected to another term as President in 1904.

Proud is the happy grief with which I sing;
  For, O my Country! in the paths of men
    There never walked a grander man than he!
He was a peer of princes—yea, a king!
    Crowned in the shambles and the prison-pen!
    The noblest Slave that ever God set free!"

Bibliography

The only original sources of information concerning the early life of Frederick Douglass are the three autobiographies published by him at various times; and the present writer, like all others who have written of Mr. Douglass, has had to depend upon this personal record for the incidents of Mr. Douglass's life in slavery. As to the second period of his life, his public career as anti-slavery orator and agitator, the sources of information are more numerous and varied. The biographies of noted abolitionists whose lives ran from time to time in parallel lines with his make very full reference to Douglass's services in their common cause, the one giving the greatest detail being the very complete and admirable *Life and Times of William Lloyd Garrison*, by his sons, which is in effect an exhaustive history of the Garrisonian movement for abolition.

The files of the *Liberator*, Mr. Garrison's paper, which can be found in a number of the principal public libraries of the country, constitute a vast storehouse of information concerning the labors of the American Anti-slavery Society, with which Douglass was identified from 1843 to 1847, the latter being the year in which he gave up his employment as agent of the society and established his paper at Rochester. Many letters from Mr. Douglass's pen appeared in the *Liberator* during this period.

Mr. Douglass's own memories are embraced in three separate volumes, published at wide intervals, each succeeding volume being a revision of the preceding work, with various additions and omissions.

I. *Narrative of Frederick Douglass. Written by himself.* (Boston, 1845: The American Anti-slavery Society.) Numerous editions of this book were printed, and translations published in Germany and in France.

II. *My Bondage and My Freedom.* (New York and Auburn, 1855: Miller, Orton & Mulligan.) This second of Mr. Douglass's autobiographies has a well-written and appreciative introduction by James M'Cune Smith and an appendix containing extracts from Mr. Douglass's speeches on slavery.

III. *Recollections of the Anti-slavery Conflict.* By Samuel J. May. (Boston, 1869: Fields, Osgood & Co.) Collected papers by a veteran abolitionist; contains an appreciative sketch of Douglass.

IV. *History of the Rise and Fall of the Slave Power in America.* By Henry Wilson. 3 vols. (Boston, 1872: James R. Osgood & Co.) The author presents an admirable summary of the life and mission of Mr. Douglass.

V. *William Lloyd Garrison and His Times.* By Oliver Johnson. (Boston, 1881: Houghton, Mifflin & Co.) One of the best works on the anti-slavery agitation, by one of its most able, active and courageous promoters.

VI. *Century Magazine,* November, 1881, "My Escape from Slavery." By Frederick Douglass.

VII. *Life and Times of Frederick Douglass.* Written by himself. (Hartford, 1882: Park Publishing Company.)

VIII. *History of the Negro Race in America.* By George W. Williams. 2 vols. (New York, 1883: G. P. Putnam's Sons.) This exhaustive and scholarly work contains an estimate of Douglass's career by an Afro-American author.

IX. *The Life and Times of Wendell Phillips.* By George Lowell Austin. (Boston, 1888: Lee & Shepard.) Contains a eulogy on Wendell Phillips by Mr. Douglass.

X. *Life and Times of William Lloyd Garrison.* By his children. 4 vols. (New York, 1889: The Century Company. London:

T. Fisher Unwin.) Here are many details of the public services of Mr. Douglass,—his relations to the Garrisonian abolitionists, his political views, his oratory, etc.

XI. *The Cosmopolitan,* August, 1889. "Reminiscences." By Frederick Douglass. In "The Great Agitation Series."

XII. *Frederick Douglass, the Colored Orator.* By Frederick May Holland. (New York, 1891: Funk & Wagnalls.) This volume is one of the series of "American Reformers," and with the exception of his own books is the only comprehensive life of Douglass so far published. It contains selections from many of his best speeches and a full list of his numerous publications.

XIII. *Our Day,* August, 1894. "Frederick Douglass as Orator and Reformer." By W. L. Garrison [(1838–1909), the first son and namesake of the Abolitionist leader (1805–1879)].

XIV. *The Underground Railroad.* By William H. Siebert. With an introduction by Albert Bushnell Hart. (New York, 1898: The Macmillan Company.) Contains many references to Mr. Douglass's services in aiding the escape of fugitive slaves.[1]

---

[1] Editor's Note to Dover Edition: *The Underground Railroad* by William Still, mentioned on page 34 (which had a subtitle different from that of the later Siebert book, listed here), was first published in 1872.

Index

This Index is primarily an index of names. The Chronology and the Bibliography have not been indexed, except in cases where a name is mentioned only in one or both of those places, or when the Chronology or the Bibliography includes information not duplicated in the main text. Nor has the material added for the 2002 edition been indexed. As Chesnutt's biography is a chronological account of Douglass's public life only, no attempt has been made to provide an index within an index by ordering all topics under an entry for Douglass, Frederick. To avoid the necessity of adding numerous editor's notes to identify individuals who were famous at some time during the years 1838–1899, but whose names will not be recognized readily by most readers in the twenty-first century, in this Index first names have been provided for people whose first name was not mentioned in Chesnutt's text. For some elected government officials, political-party affiliation and state represented have been indicated.

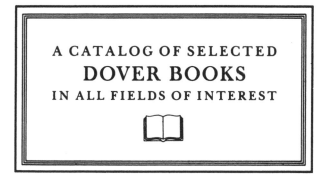

A CATALOG OF SELECTED
DOVER BOOKS
IN ALL FIELDS OF INTEREST

A CATALOG OF SELECTED DOVER
BOOKS IN ALL FIELDS OF INTEREST

CONCERNING THE SPIRITUAL IN ART, Wassily Kandinsky. Pioneering work by father of abstract art. Thoughts on color theory, nature of art. Analysis of earlier masters. 12 illustrations. 80pp. of text. $5^{3}/_{8}$ x $8^{1}/_{2}$.   0-486-23411-8

CELTIC ART: The Methods of Construction, George Bain. Simple geometric techniques for making Celtic interlacements, spirals, Kells-type initials, animals, humans, etc. Over 500 illustrations. 160pp. 9 x 12. (Available in U.S. only.)   0-486-22923-8

AN ATLAS OF ANATOMY FOR ARTISTS, Fritz Schider. Most thorough reference work on art anatomy in the world. Hundreds of illustrations, including selections from works by Vesalius, Leonardo, Goya, Ingres, Michelangelo, others. 593 illustrations. 192pp. $7^{1}/_{8}$ x $10^{1}/_{4}$.   0-486-20241-0

CELTIC HAND STROKE-BY-STROKE (Irish Half-Uncial from "The Book of Kells"): An Arthur Baker Calligraphy Manual, Arthur Baker. Complete guide to creating each letter of the alphabet in distinctive Celtic manner. Covers hand position, strokes, pens, inks, paper, more. Illustrated. 48pp. $8^{1}/_{4}$ x 11.   0-486-24336-2

EASY ORIGAMI, John Montroll. Charming collection of 32 projects (hat, cup, pelican, piano, swan, many more) specially designed for the novice origami hobbyist. Clearly illustrated easy-to-follow instructions insure that even beginning papercrafters will achieve successful results. 48pp. $8^{1}/_{4}$ x 11.   0-486-27298-2

BLOOMINGDALE'S ILLUSTRATED 1886 CATALOG: Fashions, Dry Goods and Housewares, Bloomingdale Brothers. Famed merchants' extremely rare catalog depicting about 1,700 products: clothing, housewares, firearms, dry goods, jewelry, more. Invaluable for dating, identifying vintage items. Also, copyright-free graphics for artists, designers. Co-published with Henry Ford Museum & Greenfield Village. 160pp. $8^{1}/_{4}$ x 11.   0-486-25780-0

THE ART OF WORLDLY WISDOM, Baltasar Gracian. "Think with the few and speak with the many," "Friends are a second existence," and "Be able to forget" are among this 1637 volume's 300 pithy maxims. A perfect source of mental and spiritual refreshment, it can be opened at random and appreciated either in brief or at length. 128pp. $5^{3}/_{8}$ x $8^{1}/_{2}$.   0-486-44034-6

JOHNSON'S DICTIONARY: A Modern Selection, Samuel Johnson (E. L. McAdam and George Milne, eds.). This modern version reduces the original 1755 edition's 2,300 pages of definitions and literary examples to a more manageable length, retaining the verbal pleasure and historical curiosity of the original. 480pp. $5^{3}/_{16}$ x $8^{1}/_{4}$.   0-486-44089-3

ADVENTURES OF HUCKLEBERRY FINN, Mark Twain, Illustrated by E. W. Kemble. A work of eternal richness and complexity, a source of ongoing critical debate, and a literary landmark, Twain's 1885 masterpiece about a barefoot boy's journey of self-discovery has enthralled readers around the world. This handsome clothbound reproduction of the first edition features all 174 of the original black-and-white illustrations. 368pp. $5^{3}/_{8}$ x $8^{1}/_{2}$.   0-486-44322-1

CATALOG OF DOVER BOOKS

STICKLEY CRAFTSMAN FURNITURE CATALOGS, Gustav Stickley and L. & J. G. Stickley. Beautiful, functional furniture in two authentic catalogs from 1910. 594 illustrations, including 277 photos, show settles, rockers, armchairs, reclining chairs, bookcases, desks, tables. 183pp. 6¹/₂ x 9¹/₄. 0-486-23838-5

AMERICAN LOCOMOTIVES IN HISTORIC PHOTOGRAPHS: 1858 to 1949, Ron Ziel (ed.). A rare collection of 126 meticulously detailed official photographs, called "builder portraits," of American locomotives that majestically chronicle the rise of steam locomotive power in America. Introduction. Detailed captions. xi+ 129pp. 9 x 12.
0-486-27393-8

AMERICA'S LIGHTHOUSES: An Illustrated History, Francis Ross Holland, Jr. Delightfully written, profusely illustrated fact-filled survey of over 200 American lighthouses since 1716. History, anecdotes, technological advances, more. 240pp. 8 x 10³/₄.
0-486-25576-X

TOWARDS A NEW ARCHITECTURE, Le Corbusier. Pioneering manifesto by founder of "International School." Technical and aesthetic theories, views of industry, economics, relation of form to function, "mass-production split" and much more. Profusely illustrated. 320pp. 6¹/₈ x 9¹/₄. (Available in U.S. only.) 0-486-25023-7

HOW THE OTHER HALF LIVES, Jacob Riis. Famous journalistic record, exposing poverty and degradation of New York slums around 1900, by major social reformer. 100 striking and influential photographs. 233pp. 10 x 7⁷/₈. 0-486-22012-5

FRUIT KEY AND TWIG KEY TO TREES AND SHRUBS, William M. Harlow. One of the handiest and most widely used identification aids. Fruit key covers 120 deciduous and evergreen species; twig key 160 deciduous species. Easily used. Over 300 photographs. 126pp. 5³/₈ x 8¹/₂. 0-486-20511-8

COMMON BIRD SONGS, Dr. Donald J. Borror. Songs of 60 most common U.S. birds: robins, sparrows, cardinals, bluejays, finches, more—arranged in order of increasing complexity. Up to 9 variations of songs of each species.
Cassette and manual 0-486-99911-4

ORCHIDS AS HOUSE PLANTS, Rebecca Tyson Northen. Grow cattleyas and many other kinds of orchids—in a window, in a case, or under artificial light. 63 illustrations. 148pp. 5³/₈ x 8¹/₂. 0-486-23261-1

MONSTER MAZES, Dave Phillips. Masterful mazes at four levels of difficulty. Avoid deadly perils and evil creatures to find magical treasures. Solutions for all 32 exciting illustrated puzzles. 48pp. 8¹/₄ x 11. 0-486-26005-4

MOZART'S DON GIOVANNI (DOVER OPERA LIBRETTO SERIES) Wolfgang Amadeus Mozart. Introduced and translated by Ellen H. Bleiler. Standard Italian libretto, with complete English translation. Convenient and thoroughly portable—an ideal companion for reading along with a recording or the performance itself. Introduction. List of characters. Plot summary. 121pp. 5¹/₄ x 8¹/₂. 0-486-24944-1

FRANK LLOYD WRIGHT'S DANA HOUSE, Donald Hoffmann. Pictorial essay of residential masterpiece with over 160 interior and exterior photos, plans, elevations, sketches and studies. 128pp. 9¹/₄ x 10³/₄. 0-486-29120-0

MAKING FURNITURE MASTERPIECES: 30 Projects with Measured Drawings, Franklin H. Gottshall. Step-by-step instructions, illustrations for constructing handsome, useful pieces, among them a Sheraton desk, Chippendale chair, Spanish desk, Queen Anne table and a William and Mary dressing mirror. 224pp. 8¹/₈ x 11¹/₄. 0-486-29338-6

NORTH AMERICAN INDIAN DESIGNS FOR ARTISTS AND CRAFTSPEOPLE, Eva Wilson. Over 360 authentic copyright-free designs adapted from Navajo blankets, Hopi pottery, Sioux buffalo hides, more. Geometrics, symbolic figures, plant and animal motifs, etc. 128pp. 8⅜ x 11. (Not for sale in the United Kingdom.) 0-486-25341-4

THE FOSSIL BOOK: A Record of Prehistoric Life, Patricia V. Rich et al. Profusely illustrated definitive guide covers everything from single-celled organisms and dinosaurs to birds and mammals and the interplay between climate and man. Over 1,500 illustrations. 760pp. 7¹/₂ x 10¹/₈. 0-486-29371-8

VICTORIAN ARCHITECTURAL DETAILS: Designs for Over 700 Stairs, Mantels, Doors, Windows, Cornices, Porches, and Other Decorative Elements, A. J. Bicknell & Company. Everything from dormer windows and piazzas to balconies and gable ornaments. Also includes elevations and floor plans for handsome, private residences and commercial structures. 80pp. 9⅜ x 12¹/₄. 0-486-44015-X

WESTERN ISLAMIC ARCHITECTURE: A Concise Introduction, John D. Hoag. Profusely illustrated critical appraisal compares and contrasts Islamic mosques and palaces—from Spain and Egypt to other areas in the Middle East. 139 illustrations. 128pp. 6 x 9. 0-486-43760-4

CHINESE ARCHITECTURE: A Pictorial History, Liang Ssu-ch'eng. More than 240 rare photographs and drawings depict temples, pagodas, tombs, bridges, and imperial palaces comprising much of China's architectural heritage. 152 halftones, 94 diagrams. 232pp. 10³/₄ x 9⁷/₈. 0-486-43999-2

THE RENAISSANCE: Studies in Art and Poetry, Walter Pater. One of the most talked-about books of the 19th century, *The Renaissance* combines scholarship and philosophy in an innovative work of cultural criticism that examines the achievements of Botticelli, Leonardo, Michelangelo, and other artists. "The holy writ of beauty."—Oscar Wilde. 160pp. 5³/₈ x 8¹/₂. 0-486-44025-7

A TREATISE ON PAINTING, Leonardo da Vinci. The great Renaissance artist's practical advice on drawing and painting techniques covers anatomy, perspective, composition, light and shadow, and color. A classic of art instruction, it features 48 drawings by Nicholas Poussin and Leon Battista Alberti. 192pp. 5³/₈ x 8¹/₂. 0-486-44155-5

THE ESSENTIAL JEFFERSON, Thomas Jefferson, edited by John Dewey. This extraordinary primer offers a superb survey of Jeffersonian thought. It features writings on political and economic philosophy, morals and religion, intellectual freedom and progress, education, secession, slavery, and more. 176pp. 5³/₈ x 8¹/₂. 0-486-46599-3

WASHINGTON IRVING'S RIP VAN WINKLE, Illustrated by Arthur Rackham. Lovely prints that established artist as a leading illustrator of the time and forever etched into the popular imagination a classic of Catskill lore. 51 full-color plates. 80pp. 8³/₈ x 11. 0-486-44242-X

HENSCHE ON PAINTING, John W. Robichaux. Basic painting philosophy and methodology of a great teacher, as expounded in his famous classes and workshops on Cape Cod. 7 illustrations in color on covers. 80pp. 5³/₈ x 8¹/₂. 0-486-43728-0

LIGHT AND SHADE: A Classic Approach to Three-Dimensional Drawing, Mrs. Mary P. Merrifield. Handy reference clearly demonstrates principles of light and shade by revealing effects of common daylight, sunshine, and candle or artificial light on geometrical solids. 13 plates. 64pp. 5³/₈ x 8¹/₂. 0-486-44143-1

ASTROLOGY AND ASTRONOMY: A Pictorial Archive of Signs and Symbols, Ernst and Johanna Lehner. Treasure trove of stories, lore, and myth, accompanied by more than 300 rare illustrations of planets, the Milky Way, signs of the zodiac, comets, meteors, and other astronomical phenomena. 192pp. 8⁵/₈ x 11. 0-486-43981-X

JEWELRY MAKING: Techniques for Metal, Tim McCreight. Easy-to-follow instructions and carefully executed illustrations describe tools and techniques, use of gems and enamels, wire inlay, casting, and other topics. 72 line illustrations and diagrams. 176pp. 8¹/₄ x 10⁷/₈. 0-486-44043-5

MAKING BIRDHOUSES: Easy and Advanced Projects, Gladstone Califf. Easy-to-follow instructions include diagrams for everything from a one-room house for bluebirds to a forty-two-room structure for purple martins. 56 plates; 4 figures. 80pp. 8³/₄ x 6³/₈. 0-486-44183-0

LITTLE BOOK OF LOG CABINS: How to Build and Furnish Them, William S. Wicks. Handy how-to manual, with instructions and illustrations for building cabins in the Adirondack style, fireplaces, stairways, furniture, beamed ceilings, and more. 102 line drawings. 96pp. 8³/₄ x 6³/₈. 0-486-44259-4

THE SEASONS OF AMERICA PAST, Eric Sloane. From "sugaring time" and strawberry picking to Indian summer and fall harvest, a whole year's activities described in charming prose and enhanced with 79 of the author's own illustrations. 160pp. 8¹/₄ x 11. 0-486-44220-9

THE METROPOLIS OF TOMORROW, Hugh Ferriss. Generous, prophetic vision of the metropolis of the future, as perceived in 1929. Powerful illustrations of towering structures, wide avenues, and rooftop parks—all features in many of today's modern cities. 59 illustrations. 144pp. 8¹/₄ x 11. 0-486-43727-2

THE PATH TO ROME, Hilaire Belloc. This 1902 memoir abounds in lively vignettes from a vanished time, recounting a pilgrimage on foot across the Alps and Apennines in order to "see all Europe which the Christian Faith has saved." 77 of the author's original line drawings complement his sparkling prose. 272pp. 5³/₈ x 8¹/₂. 0-486-44001-X

THE HISTORY OF RASSELAS: Prince of Abissinia, Samuel Johnson. Distinguished English writer attacks eighteenth century optimism and man's unrealistic estimates of what life has to offer. 112pp. 5³/₈ x 8¹/₂. 0-486-44094-X

A VOYAGE TO ARCTURUS, David Lindsay. A brilliant flight of pure fancy, where wild creatures crowd the fantastic landscape and demented torturers dominate victims with their bizarre mental powers. 272pp. 5³/₈ x 8¹/₂. 0-486-44198-9

Paperbound unless otherwise indicated. Available at your book dealer, online at **www.doverpublications.com**, or by writing to Dept. GI, Dover Publications, Inc., 31 East 2nd Street, Mineola, NY 11501. For current price information or for free catalogs (please indicate field of interest), write to Dover Publications or log on to **www.doverpublications.com** and see every Dover book in print. Dover publishes more than 400 books each year on science, elementary and advanced mathematics, biology, music, art, literary history, social sciences, and other areas.